The Interpretation of Art

# THE
# INTERPRETATION
# OF ART

*Essays on the Art Criticism of*

JOHN RUSKIN

WALTER PATER

CLIVE BELL

ROGER FRY

AND

HERBERT READ

*by Solomon Fishman*

UNIVERSITY OF CALIFORNI

BERKELEY AND LOS ANGELE

1963

IVERSITY OF CALIFORNIA PRESS
rkeley and Los Angeles, California

MBRIDGE UNIVERSITY PRESS
London, England

The Regents of the University of California
Congress Catalog Card Number: 63-16565

Designed by Adrian Wilson
ted in the United States of America

# Contents

# Introduction

THE question most likely to be raised concerning the essays which comprise this study is why these five writers were chosen to the exclusion of all other writers on art. The answer is partly personal. My interest in art criticism is an outgrowth of literary interests, and I was already acquainted with the work of these men through their literary associations. As a graduate student I had become familiar with Walter Pater as a literary critic and later with Herbert Read's theory of poetry in relation to his critical practice. Virginia Woolf's biography provided my first knowledge of the significance of Roger Fry. Roger Fry and Clive Bell are, of course, familiar to anyone interested in the intellectual phenomenon known as Bloomsbury, even if their works are not. Ruskin was well known to me as a monument of Victorian literature and as a progenitor of British socialism. But while I have always admired *The Stones of Venice,* I must admit that I was repelled by *Modern Painters* on first reading.

While my own introduction to aesthetics and art criticism was by way of literature, it is by no means merely fortuitous that these particular critics should also be men of letters. Readers of Henry James and Max Beerbohm can hardly be unaware of the close links between literature and painting in England from the 1880's onward. In France the rapport was even closer and more momentous. One need only recall the great preoccupation with the visual arts on the part of

I

Balzac, Stendhal, Gautier, the Goncourts, Zola, and Proust. But even more remarkable is the fact that the leading art critics in France of the nineteenth and twentieth centuries should have been Baudelaire and André Malraux. It is normal enough for the practitioner of one art to acquire an absorbing interest in another art, but in the area of criticism of the arts the writer has all the advantage over the painter insofar as criticism is a verbal craft. If the critic aspires to a public role, a minimum degree of literary skill is indispensable.

The extraordinary literary abilities with which all the subjects of this study are endowed undoubtedly account for the influence their criticism exerted in the molding of taste and the formation of public attitudes toward the visual arts. Yet none of them is a professional in the strict sense of having been trained in art history or *Kunstforschung*. (It is significant that there is no precise equivalent in English.) Nor indeed is art criticism the principal occupation of these writers. I should say that Pater's literary studies and philosophical fiction bulk larger in an over-all view of his work than does his art criticism. Ruskin's interests were multifarious; although his quasi-scientific works may now be dismissed as the product of eccentricity, his role as a social critic is no less important than his writings on art. Read is one of the most versatile writers of our time, and his reputation rests as much on his poetry and literary criticism as on his work on art. Clive Bell's interests appear to be evenly divided between literature and the visual arts. Of the group, Roger Fry comes closest to the category of the professional, having been a painter himself and having served as a museum director and an expert on the authentication of works of art. Although his contemporaries chose to regard him primarily as a critic—according to many, the greatest art critic of the twentieth century—Fry himself always regarded his criticism as secondary to his painting.

There can be little doubt that Fry's critical gifts were immeasurably enlarged by his experience as a painter. This is also true of Ruskin, who possessed extraordinary skill as a draftsman. But the practice of an art is not always an unalloyed advantage; a critic's limitations as well as his superiority may be directly attributable to it.

Having established the critic's role as mediator between the artist and the public as a central topic of this study, I have confined myself entirely to British writers. To have included continental and American writers was not only beyond my scope, but would also have involved complicated problems concerning the development of taste. Even within the limits enunciated, I can make no claim to comprehensiveness. I have not attempted to provide a history of English writing on art, nor even to discuss all its major figures. A comprehensive survey would have to include certain eighteenth-century writers, Reynolds and Hogarth on painting and possibly Shaftesbury and Burke on aesthetics. There are notable omissions in the nineteenth century—Hazlitt, William Morris, Whistler (British by virtue of residence), George Moore, and Arthur Symons. Symons, a disciple of Pater, was much more knowledgeable than his master concerning the visual arts and much more aware of important contemporary art. Yet neither he nor the others I have just mentioned was a seminal critic in the sense that Ruskin and Pater were. The same reservation can be made about important twentieth-century writers such as Sir Kenneth Clark, R. H. Wilenski, Eric Gill, and Eric Newton.

One circumstance common to the writers I am considering, which lends a certain homogeneity to this study, is a consciousness of serving as spokesmen for art to an audience that was mainly indifferent or even hostile. Not since the early Middle Ages had the English occupied a position of eminence in the visual arts, and after the Elizabethan period, which witnessed an amazing flowering of music, the English genius was preëminently literary and political. Despite the splendors of eighteenth-century English painting and architecture, various circumstances, including the rise of the middle class, the preponderance of Puritan morality, and the growth of industrialism, had contributed, by the mid-nineteenth century, to a great loss of prestige by the visual arts. Ruskin's propaganda for art was designed to demonstrate its intellectual and spiritual values—its parity with literature, so to speak. His argument on behalf of the dignity of art was mainly based on those literary, moral, and religious assumptions which were deeply ingrained in the national temper. Despite the fact that the aesthetic outlook of Pater, Fry, and Bell represents a violent reaction to Ruskin's moralistic and literary interpretation of art, they were no less concerned than he to overcome the national apathy toward art and to assert its cultural importance. Herbert Read has continued the campaign by reconciling the oppositions implicit in the work of his predecessors in an aesthetic philosophy which stresses the social and ethical values of art without sacrificing the idea of aesthetic autonomy. The work of these writers may be viewed, then, as forming a continuous and peculiarly indigenous tradition covering a span of four generations which witnessed the emergence of a highly industrialized society.

If, as I think, this body of art criticism comprises a fairly complete cycle, it would be a mistake to gauge its importance solely in terms of its local relevance, that is, to the sociology of art in England from the mid-nineteenth century to the present. It is representative of the whole development of modern art criticism and aesthetic theory, particularly as these reflect the phenomenon of modern art. Art criticism, as such, did not exist before the nineteenth century. Previously, writing on art consisted principally of technical treatises and lives of the artists. In the late eighteenth century there began to appear accounts of exhibitions which em-

bodied the personal opinions of the writers, but these belong
to the category of journalism rather than criticism. Art criticism proper began with the romantic conception of visual
art as an activity which involves the whole life of the mind,
an act of the imagination. The abandonment of classical
theories of imitation and the shift of emphasis from the concept of beauty to that of expression revolutionized both aesthetic theory and criticism. The focus of interest became the
work of art itself, and the character of aesthetic experience
was perceived to exist in its differentiation from ordinary experience. The culmination of this movement was the recognition of the formal element in art as the locus of aesthetic
experience.

Insofar as criticism is applied aesthetics, I feel justified in
devoting the major part of this study to the examination of
aesthetic theory. My task might have been easier had any
of the writers with whom I am concerned been creators of
systems, but there is nothing in English writing on art comparable to German scholarship in the nineteenth and twentieth centuries, with its thorough investigation of art history,
the psychology of perception, and the aesthetics of expression
and pure visibility. My own approach is not postulated on
any fixed set of aesthetic assumptions. Criticism is a complex
activity, involving the subtle interaction of practice and
theory. I have attempted to extract from the work of each
of these writers those theoretical assumptions which form
the basis of his critical practice and to trace the development
of aesthetic doctrine as it was modified by the critic's experience of actual works of art.

Preference and judgment count as heavily as theories of
art in the critic's role as mediator between artist and public;
in this respect, the critic's sensibility and his intuitive reactions to works of art are of prime importance. In fact, theory
may sometimes become a mere rationalization of innate predilections. Therefore, while attempting to establish the larger

pattern represented in the cycle of art criticism, I have also been concerned with the critic's individuality, his relation to the art of his time, his interests, his strength and limitations as an interpreter.

Having called into question the objectivity of critics, we should not be blind to our own prejudices. My own point of view is conditioned by what may be euphemistically called historical perspective, but which may be nothing more than prejudice. I have deliberately avoided an historicist attempt to view the nineteenth-century critics entirely in terms of their own situation and the twentieth-century critics in terms of our own. Just as we are bound to view the art of the past with contemporary eyes, we cannot avoid assessing the criticism of the previous century in terms of our own responses to art. There can be no doubt that criticism is subject to obsolescence to a far greater degree than are works of art. Hence it is almost impossible to accept the views of Ruskin and Pater at face value in view of the remarkable development of art since their time and its effect on our own standards of judgment and modes of viewing art. It will be evident that the critics examined here fall into two groups, separated by a great gulf—awareness of the modern movement. There is no general agreement concerning either the beginnings of modern art or its precise nature, but we can assume that the period of a century which embraces the work of our critics coincides with a period of art which in productivity and significance is more impressive than any other period since the Renaissance. At the time he wrote the first volume of *Modern Painters,* Ruskin knew the work of Turner and the English landscape school, but his knowledge of European art was limited to the works purchased by his father and those he saw in the National Gallery. Although he was to expand his knowledge of Italian painting enormously in the following decades by annual visits to the Continent, he remained totally indifferent during his whole career to French painting, particularly the work of his own time which constitutes the foundation of modern art. There were great areas of the art of the past which were completely unknown to nineteenth-century critics, including almost all forms of primitive and exotic art which have been rediscovered in the twentieth century. Pater's range of knowledge was even more limited than Ruskin's, being confined to Greek sculpture and the painting of the Italian Renaissance. While there is some indirect evidence of Pater's interest in contemporary art, it plays no part in his criticism.

The most radical development in modern art and, according to its proponents, the rational culmination of the whole movement, occurred long after the time of Ruskin and Pater. I refer, of course, to abstract or nonrepresentational art in its many manifestations. The problem of representation had been extremely important in nineteenth-century aesthetics, but the discussion had been conducted entirely within the context of representational art. The crux of twentieth-century criticism and theory is the issue of nonrepresentational art itself. Although Roger Fry and Clive Bell held advanced views on the subject of representation in art, they manifested little interest in abstract art or sympathy with it. To Herbert Read, who has been a most active apologist for the radical art of this century, the formalist aesthetics of Bell and Fry appears to be reactionary. To a certain extent, the division of twentieth-century critics into two groups is chronological, since Read belongs to a succeeding generation. There are more fundamental doctrinal differences between them, however, and it is unlikely that Roger Fry would have approved of Abstract Expressionism and Action Painting had he lived to witness them.

The essays which compose this volume are conceived, then, as forming parts of a larger whole which is the study of developing modes of aesthetic consciousness and attitudes toward art during a period which was overwhelmingly devoted to material and practical values and in a country whose culture was oriented toward the intellectual and the moral rather than toward the aesthetic. In one respect, at least, the pedagogical aspect of English art criticism was attended by success. There is plenty of evidence that the provincial status of British art is a thing of the past; the contemporary "renaissance" in painting and sculpture must be attributed in part to the existence of a public no less receptive to art than those in other countries in which art flourishes. Although they display great diversity in ideas and taste, all the critics dealt with here were instrumental in shaping the response of the public, first of all toward art in general, and finally toward modern art. Taken as a whole, their work represents a single segment of the total enterprise undertaken by men to understand and illuminate art, and as such it provides interest for anyone who wishes to enlarge his own understanding.

I have provided for each essay a brief chronology which, in addition to the significant dates, lists the principal works of each critic and refers to events relevant to his career as a critic.

# JOHN RUSKIN

1819  Born in London, February 8, the only son of James Ruskin, a wine merchant, who had married his cousin, Margaret Cox. Ruskin was a precocious, solitary child, subjected to extremes of adulation and restraint on the part of his parents. His earliest education was undertaken by his mother, who had dedicated him to God before his birth. His father was a highly cultivated man, an amateur artist, a collector of art, and a lover of poetry.

1823  His parents purchased a house at Herne Hill, a rural village near Dulwich. Between the ages of five and fourteen, he read the Bible daily with his mother. At the age of eight he began to write verse; at ten he began lessons from a drawing master; in the following year he took up the study of Greek with a private tutor. Ruskin was a voracious reader as a child; he also wrote voluminously—verses, dramas, romances. He accompanied his parents on his father's annual business trips in Britain, visiting country houses, castles, churches, and art collections.

1832  Received a copy of Rogers' *Italy,* illustrated by Turner and others, as a birthday gift. Made exact copies of the Turner drawings. This volume was decisive in shaping Ruskin's interests.

1833  First trip to Continent with his parents, visiting France, Switzerland, and Italy. Made many landscape sketches and drawings. On his return to England was sent to a private school conducted by Rev. Thomas Dale. Privately tutored in French and mathematics.

1834 First published works: "On the Causes of the Colour of the Water of the Rhine" and "The Strata of Mont Blanc," *Magazine of Natural History*, London.

1835 Attended lectures on early English literature at King's College, London; received lessons in water color drawing from Copley Fielding.

1836 Saw three Turners at the Royal Academy. An unfavorable review of Turner's work in *Blackwoods' Magazine* raised him to a "height of black anger." Spent summer abroad. Discovered architecture, but his interests were chiefly scientific—geology and meteorology. Remarkable prose descriptions of landscape in his journal.

1837 Entered Christ Church, Oxford, as a gentleman commoner. His parents wished him to enter the clergy. His mother moved to Oxford in order to supervise his life and health. His chief intellectual interest was verse writing.

1837– "The Poetry of Architecture" and "The British Villa" pub-
1838 lished in the *Architectural Magazine*.

1839 Won the Newdigate Prize for Poetry.

1840 Met Turner. Contracted tuberculosis and went to Italy with his parents for his health. Discovered in Rome that he did not have the requisite gifts to become a professional artist. Planned a book in defence of Turner. Wrote *The King of the Golden River*, a fairy tale, for Euphemia Gray, a distant cousin.

1841 Took his B.A. at Oxford. Toured France, Switzerland, and Germany with his parents. Renounced a clerical career.

1842 Parents purchased a house at Denmark Hill. Ruskin began work on a book on Turner. Spent summer in Chamonix in order to study the rock formations of Mont Blanc.

1843 *Modern Painters,* volume I, published anonymously. It was better received in the literary world than by artists and professional writers on art. Took M.A. degree at Oxford.

1844 To Switzerland with parents. Studied sunsets, made precise drawings of plants, lichens, clouds, and rocks.

1845 Traveled to Italy alone for the first time. This was the most memorable journey of his life. He realized for the first time the supremacy of early Italian art—Cimabue, Orcagna, Ghirlandajo, Giotto, Fra Angelico. Discovered Tintoretto in Venice. Made many careful studies of architectural subjects.

1848 Married Euphemia Chalmers Gray. The marriage was never consummated, and was obviously ill-fated from the start. The couple lived in Ruskin's parental house after their return from a wedding trip to the Continent. Ruskin's interests turned to architecture.

1849 Published *The Seven Lamps of Architecture,* illustrated by himself. Spent nearly a year in Venice in preparation of *The Stones of Venice.*

1851 Published *The Stones of Venice,* volume I; published the *Construction of Sheepfolds,* a pamphlet advocating union between Protestant Anglicans and Dissenters; defended the Pre-Raphaelite painters in a letter to *The Times;* began to lose his faith in dogmatic religion. Became interested in contemporary socioeconomic problems.

1853 Published second and third volumes of *The Stones of Venice.* Spent several weeks at Glenfilas in Scotland with the painter, John Everett Millais. Ruskin had great success as a lecturer on art in Edinburgh.

1854– Marriage annulled. A year later, Effie married Millais.
1855 Ruskin formed friendships with Carlyle and with Dante Gabriel Rosetti, to whom he gave financial assistance. Toured Switzerland with his parents. On his return participated in the foundation of the Working Men's College in Red Lion Square, London, with F. D. Maurice. Ruskin undertook instruction in art. Published first of a series of *Academy Notes.*

1856– Published the third and fourth volumes of *Modern Paint-*
1857 *ers,* and *Elements of Drawing.* Trip to Switzerland. Formed friendship with Charles Eliot Norton.

1857 Began to catalogue the works of Turner in the National Gallery. Gave lectures in Manchester on "The Political Economy of Art."

1858 Met Rose La Touche, then nine years old, with whom he fell violently and tragically in love.

1860 Published three articles on taxation, suffrage, and education in *Cornhill Magazine* under the editorship of Thackeray; eventually published as *Unto This Last,* these articles formed the basis of Ruskin's political and economic doctrine. Published fifth volume of *Modern Painters.*

1863 Published political articles in *Fraser's Magazine,* later collected under the title *Munera Pulveris.* Became interested in a girl's school at Winnington, which he frequently visited.

1864 Death of father. Delivered lectures at Manchester, later published as *Sesame and Lilies.*

1865– Published *Ethics of the Dust,* dialogues with imaginary
1866 girls; *The Crown of Wild Olive,* lectures on war, industry, education, and honor. Proposed marriage to Rose La Touche, but was refused.

1867  Published *Time and Tide;* delivered Rede Lecture at Cambridge on "The Relation of National Ethics to National Art."

1869  Published *The Queen of the Air,* lectures on Greek myths; was appointed Slade Professor of Art at Oxford.

1870  Gave his first lectures as Slade Professor. Began *Fors Clavigera,* a series of letters to workingmen on a wide variety of topics which were issued in monthly installments until 1884. Studied the work of Carpaccio in Venice. Wrote *Aratra Pentelici* (published 1872), a series of lectures on Greek coins and sculpture. Death of his mother. Bought Brantwood on Coniston Lake, which was to be his home for the rest of his life.

1871  Formed the Company of St. George, a lay guild of persons pledged to put into practice Ruskin's economic and social doctrines.

1872  Started a street-sweeping project in London. Published *The Eagle's Nest.*

1873  Published *Ariadne Florentina,* his Oxford lectures on Botticelli and Florentine engraving.

1874  Started the Hinksey road-building project with his students, among whom were Arnold Toynbee, Oscar Wilde, Andrew Lang, Alfred Milner, and Alexander Wedderburn; refused gold medal of Royal Institute of British Architects. Published the *Laws of Fiesole,* a course in drawing designed for undergraduates. Took trip to Italy, where he made studies for *Mornings in Florence.* Rose La Touche suffered a final attack of madness.

1875  Death of Rose La Touche. Published *Proserpina,* a study of flowers, and *Deucalion,* studies in geology.

1877  Published *Guide to the Academy at Venice* and *St. Mark's Rest*. Wrote a vicious attack on one of Whistler's paintings in *Fors Clavigera*. Whistler retaliated by suing Ruskin for libel. In a court trial which received enormous publicity, Ruskin was found guilty and fined one shilling. As a consequence of the trial, Ruskin resigned his professorship.

1878  Suffered his first attack of madness, which lasted six weeks.

1880  Trip to France. Began work on *The Bible of Amiens*. Published *The Elements of Prosody*.

1881– Three further attacks of mental illness.
1882

1883  Was reëlected to Slade Professorship. Lectured on the art of England.

1884  Two lectures at the London Institute on *The Storm Cloud of the Nineteenth Century*. Much occupied with crystallography.

1885  Resigned his professorship, ostensibly on the issue of vivisection. Began work on his autobiography, *Praeterita*. Suffered another attack of mental illness. Recovery was incomplete. Ruskin College for Working Men established at Oxford.

1885– Spent his remaining years at Brantwood, where he con-
1900  tinued to work on *Praeterita* during his intermittent periods of clarity. Died January 21, 1900.

OF all writers on art, Ruskin is the most difficult to evaluate today. The critics of the second and third decades of this century who were preoccupied with the absorption and naturalization of modern art, ranged him with the enemy, the reactionary opponents of modern art.

In those years his reputation reached its lowest point; he was anathema to all who regarded modern art as a liberation from the tyranny of subject matter, from literal representation, and above all from subservience to social or ethical standards or judgments. The low estimate of Ruskin was part of a whole generation's rejection of Victorian idols, and it is entirely natural that some restitution has been undertaken by the following generation. But it is unlikely that his reputation can ever be fully rehabilitated or that the bulk of his writings on art can mean very much to the contemporary reader. The difficulties of Ruskin's work are of two kinds. The first, which have been ably demonstrated by R. H. Wilenski and Joan Evans, are related to his mental constitution, to serious psychological disturbances, and to a fundamental incapacity for sustained intellectual production. The second stem from Ruskin's historical situation, from his relation to the art and to the art theories of his age; some of the unresolved contradictions in Ruskin's views on art are not, as has been claimed, merely the inconsistencies of a man of genius who could afford to transcend the limits of logic observed by lesser minds. They are involved in the dilemma which confronted the visual arts throughout the whole of the nineteenth century and which culminated in the superseding of Impressionism by modern art at the end of the century.

The contradiction most striking to readers who have grown up in the climate of twentieth-century art and art theory is Ruskin's insistence on visual truth as the basic criterion of artistic excellence while at the same time advocating art as the product of the imagination and as an expression of the human spirit. Thus, Ruskin's extravagant enthusiasm for Turner's pictures is based on an intuitive recognition of their imaginative force, but his defense of Turner is argued on the grounds of their representational accuracy, their fidelity to the "facts of nature."

The ambiguities of a theory which appears to place equal stress on both the mimetic and expressive functions of art can be accounted for by Ruskin's peculiar place in the overall development of aesthetics: his work is the last of a series as well as the beginning of a new series. E. H. Gombrich calls *Modern Painters* "the last and most persuasive book in the tradition that starts with Pliny and Vasari in which the history of art is interpreted as progress toward visual truth." [1] According to the prevailing doctrine of our own time, which posits the virtually total irrelevance of representational accuracy to aesthetic value, this aspect of Ruskin's work is not only reactionary but worthless. Yet in his time Ruskin's views on representation were radical; emphasizing the primacy of visual impressions as against conceptual knowledge, his arguments for observation based on the trained sensibility prefigure the doctrines of Impressionism.

The idea of close observation of nature as opposed to reliance on convention is not at all inconsistent with the romantic theory of art, but when we designate Ruskin as its first and perhaps greatest exponent in the field of the visual arts, we do not think of his views on visual truth but of his conception of art as expression:

Art is valuable . . . only as it expresses the personality, activity, and living perception of a good and great human soul . . . it may express and contain this with little help from execution, and less from science . . . if it have not this, if it show not the vigour, perception, and invention of a mighty human spirit, it is worthless.[2]

No writer in English had discussed the visual arts in such terms before; as Graham Hough has observed, Ruskin did for the painter's imagination what Coleridge had done for the poet's—"exalted it into one of the central and dominating seats in the hierarchy of human faculties." [3] By asserting the prior claims of the imaginative life over those of practical life, Ruskin endowed the visual arts with a new importance and prepared the ground for the aesthetic revolution which took place in the next hundred years, culminating in Malraux's celebration of the autonomy of modern art, "now triumphantly a law unto itself." Ruskin himself would not have sanctioned the idea of aesthetic autonomy, which in one form or another is a central tenet of all the other critics who are discussed in this book; his work nevertheless marks the start of a cycle to which all of them belong.

On the occasion of Ruskin's death, the Vice-President of the Royal Institute of British Architects, whose disinterestedness is beyond doubt, since Ruskin had done nothing in his lifetime to ingratiate himself with architects, stated what was almost universally believed: "He was the man who probably first awakened the English people to a knowledge of what art really meant: art in the life of the people, art in the true sense of the word, as an ennobling faculty which raised men and induced in them a longing for higher and nobler things." [4] The style of the eulogy, an echo of Ruskin's own idiom, partly elucidates his almost total disrepute in the following decades. For Roger Fry, Ruskin was "that old fraud. . . . He was too virtuous. Everything had to be squared— even those finicky palaces must be morally good." [5] It was Ruskin's ethical tone that alienated not only the twentieth-century reader but even the critics of his own time, and indeed Ruskin's passionate concern for art led him into exaggerations and excesses which provide an easy target for ridicule. But the real obstacle to a perception of Ruskin's value as a critic is not simply distaste for his moralism, but a fundamental discontinuity in ways of viewing works of art which separates all critics who wrote before 1900 and those who have written since. The discontinuity goes deeper than any disagreement concerning critical theory. It involves the success of modern art, a phenomenon too complex to reduce to any simple formula, but one which has at least clarified the mode of existence of works of art to the extent that the hypothetical choice posed by Ruskin in *Modern Painters* now appears absurd: "If, for instance, we could behold the Magdalene receiving her pardon at Christ's feet ... as if some silver mirror had been miraculously commanded to retain forever the colours that had flashed upon it for an instant ... would we not part with our picture, Titian's or Veronese's though it might be?"[6] It was the mimetic principle in Ruskin's criticism, far more than his ethical bias, which led Fry to associate the aesthetic heritage of Ruskin with the philistinism of the English public enraged by the first Post-Impressionist exhibition in 1910.

In order to judge Ruskin's criticism objectively we must make allowance for certain inevitable limitations in his knowledge. He could not have experienced twentieth-century modern art, and his actual experience was confined to a single tradition—that of Western art beginning with fifth-century Greek art, a small segment of medieval art, and principally of Renaissance and post-Renaissance painting through the eighteenth century. Yet, viewed in the total perspective of the history of art criticism, Ruskin's achievement is very great. Unhampered by the Englishman's prejudice against Ruskin's Victorian traits, Lionello Venturi in his *History of Art Criticism* attributes the peculiar merit of Ruskin's criticism to its origin in a genuine sensibility, to an empirical response to the manifestations of art which outweighs the ethical and religious interpretations to which this experience was subjected. In Venturi's opinion the emotive quality of Ruskin's religion did not constrict but actually reinforced his intuitive response to art, thereby preserving it from the dangers of arid intellectualism. As a follower of Croce, Venturi understandably attributes greater importance to Ruskin's intuitive insights than to his aesthetics. Ruskin is designated, along with Baudelaire, as an initiator of modern art criticism.

For Herbert Read, a professed romantic, Ruskin is not

only the greatest English art critic, but the greatest English critic of any kind. Read's estimate, like Venturi's, is based on the quality of Ruskin's sensibility, his capacity for a direct sensuous and emotional response to art linked with an extraordinary gift for communicating that response in prose, rather than on his achievement as a theorist. There is a profound affinity in Ruskin's and Read's approach to art. They are both "philosophical" critics, in Read's sense of the term, in that they are concerned with art in relation to the whole of man's experience. Allowing for the large divergences that were bound to occur in the century that separates them, we can say that their essential interest is the relation of art and society. They are both unalterably opposed to the view that aesthetic experience is so specialized or rare that it can only be of concern to a small segment of society. Consequently they address themselves to the widest possible audience.

Certainly nothing like *Modern Painters* and *The Stones of Venice* had ever appeared in England, or elsewhere in Europe. Before their appearance, art criticism had been confined to technical treatises, the lives of the painters, and, beginning with the late eighteenth century, to journalistic accounts of exhibitions. It had been directed either to the painter himself or to the connoisseur. While Ruskin was not modest about his own expert knowledge, his aim was nothing less than to convert the English public to a love of art, to share his own passionate reaction to the world of beautiful objects. The premises of his criticism—that art is a subject of importance and that it is important to everyone—were far removed from the conception of the visual arts as the special preserve of the aristocracy or as a cultural adornment of the educated classes. Ruskin must be credited with establishing the tone of modern art criticism. For him art was not a recreation: "It must be understood and undertaken seriously or not at all." [7] Although the romantic expressionist doctrine appears to stand at the opposite pole from the views of for-

malism, the formalist critics of the present century accept
Ruskin's general premise concerning art as a spiritual activity, hence as a subject of importance.

Ruskin's interest in art coincided with the composition of
the five volumes *Modern Painters,* a period beginning in
1841 and ending in 1860. During this period also appeared
*The Seven Lamps of Architecture* and *The Stones of Venice,*
which are still primarily concerned with art, but which reveal the shift in interest from art as expression to the social
conditioning of art, a shift which was to determine Ruskin's
eventual career as a social critic. There can be little doubt
concerning R. H. Wilenski's assertion that after this period
Ruskin was actually bored by art. His views and tastes had
been formulated, his responses were automatic, he was no
longer capable of "seeing" pictures. Ironically, it was only
after 1860 that his popular reputation began to grow; when
his critical abilities began to decline, he discovered a huge
audience receptive to his pontifications on art. Yet even the
work of his prime is not easy either to assimilate or to assess.
The first two volumes of *Modern Painters* are ostensibly a
vindication of Turner and a refutation of the charge of certain reviewers that his mature works were "out of nature,"
that is, a falsification of nature. Ruskin's argument on behalf
of Turner is extremely confusing, since it is conducted from
what appears to be contradictory points of view. On the one
hand, his reply to the specific charge of the critics is a dem-
onstration of the fact that Turner's work is founded upon
a knowledge of natural phenomena far superior to that of
his predecessors in landscape—Claude, Canaletto, Gaspard
Poussin, and Salvator Rosa. To mere conceptual knowledge
of these phenomena, Ruskin opposed the fresh, immediate
evidence of the senses. Ruskin was attacking the idea of academic art, an art based on rules, conventions, formulas. In
Ruskin's day the academic ideal meant specifically the tradition of the High Renaissance, of which Raphael was the

culmination. On the other hand, Ruskin's passion for Turner's work is obviously based on emotive response to its imaginative and expressive power rather than to its representational accuracy. Ruskin is moved by Turner's "poetry" rather than by his "science," and he places Turner's imagination on a par with Shakespeare's. It is on these grounds that Ruskin attacks the Dutch landscape school, including Ruysdael, Hobbema, Cuyp, Berghem, and Teniers, which in contrast to Turner, is guilty of a pedestrian realism. The dual criteria which Ruskin applies to Turner result in what appear to us as completely arbitrary judgments of other painters. One might have expected Constable to rate high on the score of visual truth in view of his influence on the Impressionists; in fact, Ruskin depreciates Constable as excessively literal. On the other hand, he praises the Pre-Raphaelite painters for the literal accuracy of detail in their work. It must be allowed that Ruskin's support of the Pre-Raphaelites was not wholly unequivocal; he regarded them as beginners rather than as masters. A main principle of his views on art education was that the novice must confine himself to an exact transcription of nature.

When confronted with the charge of inconsistency, Ruskin invariably asserts the primacy of imagination over technique conceived of as representational skill. The latter is simply the means to an end. But the problem of expression versus imitation is not thereby resolved, since for Ruskin there is no question of imaginative expression entirely superseding visual truth as it does in modern expressionist theory. To Ruskin the greatest art—imaginative art—is primarily an intensification of that truth. In the light of recent experimental psychology, visual truth is a matter of the utmost complexity and ambiguity which has so far eluded formulation. Though Ruskin's notions of perception were based on the relatively sophisticated psychology of the previous century, he did not doubt that the painter could present the "unadulterated truth of natural optics." Since, according to Ruskin, imaginative power in the visual arts is not only unteachable but also inexplicable, it must be itself regarded as some sort of natural phenomenon. Hence both the expressionist and impressionist aspects of his aesthetics are subsumed under a naturalist creed which was the chief feature of a highly personal religion.

Although *Modern Painters* had its inception in the defense of Turner against his detractors, the work rapidly outgrew that limited and, we may add, entirely meritorious aim. In order to justify Turner, Ruskin believes it necessary to set forth, once and for all, not only the principles of landscape painting but a total rationale of art, a task which would have intimidated a more mature and more knowledgeable critic. But what Ruskin lacked in experience, he made up for in aplomb and energy. The first two volumes, the first devoted mainly to "ideas of truth," the second to "ideas of beauty," constitute Ruskin's only venture into the field of abstract aesthetics and form the basis of all his future writing on art. Despite the elaborate system of classification and the paraphernalia of the formal treatise, the volumes must be judged as failures from the point of view of logic and coherence. Ruskin's system has the merit of originality; it is almost entirely nonderivative, the product of an astonishing mental effort. But his generalizations are based on a very limited although intense knowledge of painting. His indifference to existing scholarship and his failure to perceive individual works of art in relation to the history and development of art have undermined the value of his system of aesthetics for the modern reader, who finds it arbitrary to the point of eccentricity. Furthermore, Ruskin's native gifts as a writer fail to redeem it. The fertility of his mind and the fecundity of his prose make it long-winded to the point of exhaustion. Despite the classifications, divisions, and marginal summaries, it remains extremely difficult.

The systematic approach was abandoned in the third, fourth, and fifth volumes of *Modern Painters*. The heading of one of the sections of the third volume, "Of Many Things," is symptomatic of all of them. The bulk of the fourth volume is a disquisition on the structure of mountains based on early journals of travels in Switzerland. While these pages have a certain literary interest as exhibitions of a new genre—word paintings, or prose rhapsodies on natural scenery—it is difficult to perceive their relevance to the visual arts. The digressions in *Modern Painters* are in themselves a clue to the gulf which separates it from the modern consciousness of art. Although Ruskin was gifted with great powers of observation and description and therefore capable of an exhaustive, empirical description of pictorial elements unprecedented in previous writing on art, the discussion of specific works of art occupies only a small fraction of the whole work.

Despite its obvious shortcomings as a unified treatise, *Modern Painters* abounds in insights both brilliant and profound. After long stretches during which one is irritated by what, to present modes of thinking, is Ruskin's perverse insistence on literal realism, he suddenly reveals that what he really means is the transcendence of these facts. Not only does Ruskin anticipate, in theory at least, symbolism and abstraction, but he is remarkably perceptive concerning the importance of color as a formal or plastic element in painting. His exposition of Turner's treatment of light prefigures the theories of the Impressionists. His views on the unconscious nature of the imagination and on organic form as the basis of aesthetic judgment are surprisingly modern. From a work so extensive, compounded of close observation, closely reasoned exposition and argument, and pure speculation, it is possible to extract passages that could serve to illustrate a wide variety of theories. Far from being the embodiment of a mature point of view, it is actually a record of a long education in art and of the expansion of Ruskin's taste, first to admiration of the Venetians, particularly Tintoretto; then to the Italian "primitives," Cimabue, Orcagna, Ghirlandajo, Giotto, Fra Angelico; and eventually to the Pre-Raphaelites.

Ruskin was willing to admit that his statements on art were sometimes contradictory, but not that they lacked unity. But as Joan Evans has observed, his conviction of the unity of his work was a delusion: "He was apt to take his own psyche—temperament, tastes, interests, enthusiasms, sensibilities—and without much real generalization but with much oratory to make it appear of universal significance. His idea of unity was no more than the unity of his own personality." [8] The central paradox in his aesthetic theory, involving the contrary claims of imitation and expression, can be attributed to the age. The ambiguities of Ruskin's theory were augmented by preoccupations which were mainly personal and individual. His career presents the tragic spectacle of a gifted temperament and sensibility harnessed to a sense of guilt concerning his natural propensities. His writings on art were motivated by the impulse to communicate an almost hypersensitive response to sensuous beauty, whether in works of art or in the physical universe and also by a powerful urge to preach, which in Ruskin took the wholly admirable form of a strong social conscience. Before *Modern Painters* was complete, he had discovered that this double motive was really one. What had begun as a desire to convert his countrymen to his own enthusiasm for Turner, to make them *see* his pictures, ended as desire to convert them to a way of life favorable to the production of great works of art. But from the very first the legacy of a puritanical upbringing had led him to distrust aesthetic experience, to minimize and even to deny its sensuous content, and to stress its intellectual and moral implications. A symptom of this view was his substitution of the term "theoria" for "aesthetics": "The Theoretic faculty . . . is concerned with the moral perception and ap-

preciation of ideas of beauty. . . . And the error respecting
it is, the considering and calling it Aesthetic, degrading it
to a mere operation of sense." [9]

Ruskin, of course, was an aesthete in the literal sense of the
term and the progenitor of a whole school of aesthetes. But
disinterested aesthetic emotion, which later critics were to
glorify as the sole end of art, was inexplicable to Ruskin:
"There is a strong instinct in me which I cannot analyse to
draw and describe the things I love—not for reputation, nor
for the good of others, nor for my own advantage, but a sort
of instinct like that for eating and drinking. I should like to
draw all St. Marks, and all this Verona stone by stone, to
eat it all up into my mind, touch by touch." [10] Revelations
such as these were made privately. They would have been
unseemly in an author of whom George Eliot wrote: "I ven-
erate him as one of the great teachers of the day. The grand
doctrines of truth and sincerity in art, and the nobleness and
solemnity of our human life, which he teaches with the in-
spiration of a Hebrew prophet, must be stirring up young
minds in a promising way." [11] Marcel Proust, who had wor-
shiped Ruskin before his ultimate disillusionment, detects in
the very profession of these doctrines a failure in sincerity,
the result of self-deception:

The doctrines he professed were moral, not aesthetic, yet he chose
them for their beauty. And because he did not wish to present
them formally as things of beauty, but as statements of truth, he
was forced to lie to himself about the reasons that had led him to
adopt them. And once the start was made, he found himself involved in a compromise with conscience so continuous, that im-
moral doctrines sincerely professed would perhaps have been less
dangerous to his spiritual integrity than moral doctrines enunciated with less than sincerity, because they had been dictated by
aesthetic considerations which he refused to admit. Nor was the
sin occasional. It went on all the time—in the way he explained
a fact or appraised a work of art. . . . [12]

There was one manifestation of beauty about which Ruskin need not have had moral qualms—"that peculiar sensibility to the beautiful in all things that God has made which it is my present aim to render more universal." [13] Whatever guilt he may have sensed in his addiction to man-made beauty was absent in his love of nature. It is not easy to discuss the precise character of what I have called Ruskin's naturalism, since it is compounded of several elements—theological, scientific, and aesthetic—and since it was subject to modifications determined in part by his successive enthusiasms in art. As Graham Hough has suggested, the critical stages in Ruskin's religious thought were closely connected with his artistic experience. Ruskin's feeling for nature which is intimately allied, if not identical with, that acute sensibility to visual phenomena by which his art criticism is distinguished may be construed quite justly as a product of romanticism. But whereas Wordsworth's pantheism embraces human sentience and provides for a fusion of subject and object, Ruskin's theology is an idiosyncratic compound of literal pietism and an anthropocentric conception of physical nature as the handiwork of God.

Though ultimately modified, the religious view that pervades the first two volumes of *Modern Painters* is colored by a profound conviction of man's unworthiness, directly at odds with romantic individualism. Ruskin's deification of nature had important consequences for his aesthetic theory, since it heightened the disparity between expression and imitation:

Nothing can atone for the want of truth, not the most brilliant imagination, the most playful fancy, the most pure feeling; not the most exalted conception, nor the most comprehensive grasp of intellect, can make amends for the want of truth . . . because Nature is so immeasurably superior to all that the human mind can conceive, that every departure from her is a fall beneath her. . . . All falsehood must be a blot as well as a sin, an injury as well as a deception.[14]

The insistence on truth rather than expressiveness or beauty as the prime aesthetic criterion probably served to alleviate Ruskin's personal difficulties by reconciling his aesthetic experience with his conscience, but it caused irreparable damage to the intellectual fabric of his work as an art critic.

Acute sensibility to visual phenomena, his greatest asset as a writer on art, was cultivated by a lifelong devotion to scientific pursuits and to drawing. Concerning the latter, Ruskin was overly modest when he claimed in the Epilogue to *The Stones of Venice* that attainments such as his were within the reach of anyone willing to devote sufficient time, care, and exertion. While his architectural drawings and his copies of pictorial details were no more than accurate and faithful studies, his landscapes, though quite conventional, display great charm and delicacy. His graphic talent was important not only as an adjunct to his art criticism, enabling him in an era before photography to illustrate his own works, but as a formative influence in his response to art. Like those of Roger Fry, Ruskin's descriptions of works of art are based on direct observation of their visual constituents. This capacity is not equivalent to critical ability since it is shared by the connoisseur and the expert. But if the critic who is also a practitioner has certain advantages in technical knowledge and insight into the problems of artistic production, these advantages are equivocal, since the critic's ideas are unconsciously shaped by the practicing eye and hand. Fry's limitations as a critic, I believe, were partly determined by his career as a painter; to a lesser extent, Ruskin's skill as an illustrator influenced his views on art.

Ruskin's love of nature preceded his love of art. The habit of drawing and sketching acquired in boyhood, which led eventually to his passion for art and architecture, was originally connected with the interests of a naturalist. While Ruskin was to compose his own kind of nature poetry in a rhythmic prose with powerful emotional overtones, his scientific knowledge far exceeds that of Wordsworth, for instance. The drawings, however, record the careful observations of the trained naturalist rather than his emotions. Now Ruskin was well aware that the aims of science and art were not identical. Turner's achievement, if nothing else, was sufficient to demonstrate the emotive nature of great art. Yet, Ruskin cannot believe in the excellence of Claude and Poussin, whose knowledge of tree forms and foliage was obviously inferior to his own.

At best, the terms *nature* and *truth* are impossibly ambiguous in aesthetic discourse. The twentieth century has elected to discard them by choosing, perhaps too arbitrarily, to regard the problem of representation as irrelevant not only to modern art, but retroactively, to the art of the past. This doctrine is based on the assumption that the significant art of the past was covertly or unconsciously concerned with the problems of form or expression which are fully and consciously recognized in modern art. Had Ruskin's sole contribution to aesthetics consisted in a naïve naturalism, it would be easy to dismiss his views as obsolete, but his mimetic concept of art is inextricably bound up with a form of romantic expressionism which is very much alive in present-day aesthetics.

Ruskin's disapproval of imitative art as such in *Modern Painters,* volume I, might be interpreted as signifying a repudiation of the mimetic principle. The following statement could well serve as a defense of expressionist or symbolist art:

The word Truth, as applied to art, signifies the faithful statement, either to the mind or senses, of any fact of nature. (1) Imitation can only be of something material, but truth has reference to statements both of the qualities of material things, and of emotions, impressions and thoughts. There is a moral as well as a material truth, a truth of impression as well as of form, of thought as well as of matter; and the truth of impression and thought is a thousand times more important. (2) Truth may be stated by any sign or symbols which have a definite signification in the minds of those to whom they are addressed, although such signs have themselves no image nor likeness of anything. Whatever can excite in the mind the conception of certain facts, can give ideas of truth, though it be in no degree the imitation or resemblance of those facts. If there be—we do not say there is—but if there be in painting anything which operates as words do, not by resembling anything, but by being taken as a symbol and substitute for it, and thus inducing the effect of it, then this channel of communication can convey uncorrupted truth, though it do not in any degree resemble the facts whose conception it induces. . . . (3) An idea of truth exists in the statement of one attribute of anything, but an idea of imitation requires the resemblance of as many attributes as we are usually cognizant of in its real presence . . . finally, ideas of truth are the foundation and ideas of imitation, the destruction of art.[15]

Actually *imitation* in this context refers not to realistic art but to illusionist art, to *trompe l'oeil,* regarded as a mechanical trick. The statement as a whole is inconsistent neither with romantic or Impressionist principles; in practice, however, Ruskin was inclined to identify his own sense impressions with the objective "facts of nature," that is, with truth. For he conceded to no one, not even to Turner, a greater knowledge of both the inner structure and the external appearance of natural objects. Thus the criterion of fidelity to nature was invoked to justify his intuitive preferences in art, which displayed considerable deviations from any single standard of visual truth. Just as Ruskin's ideal artist is a combination of the naturalist's eye and brain and the poet's soul, his own criticism is an unstable amalgam of analytical observation and intuitive judgment.

The aspect of Ruskin's art theory most compatible with

modern aesthetics is his doctrine of imagination. Its exposition in *Modern Painters,* volume II, is extremely elaborate, involving first an absolute distinction from fancy or fantasy, which signifies the mere rearrangement or juggling of the external attributes of natural phenomena, and proceeding to the classification of imagination into three categories—penetrative, associative, and contemplative. Of these, the first alone is essential, and Ruskin's description of it is one of the central documents in the aesthetics of romanticism:

Such is always the mode in which the highest imaginative faculty seizes its materials. It never stops at crusts or ashes, or outward images of any kind; it ploughs them all aside, and plunges into the very central fiery heart; nothing else will content its spirituality; whatever semblances and outward shows and phases its subject may possess go for nothing; it gets within all fence, cuts down to the root, and drinks the very vital sap of what it deals with: once therein it is at liberty to throw up what new shoots it will, and to prune and twist them at its pleasure, and bring them to a fairer fruit than grew on the old tree; but all this pruning and twisting is work that it likes not, and often does ill; its function and gift are the getting at the root, its nature and dignity depend on its holding things always by the heart. Take its hand from off the beating of that, and it will prophesy no longer; it looks not on the eyes, it judges not by the voice, it describes not by outward features; all that it affirms, judges, or describes, it affirms from within.[16]

This aspect of Ruskin's theory is revolutionary in that it repudiates the rationalism of the neo-classic doctrine of nature "corrected" or idealized. It is essentially the intuitive character of imagination which enables the artist to grasp the inner truth of phenomena. The "inner truth," furthermore, would appear to endow the imagination not only with a cognitive function, but with a formal one transforming external sense impressions into meaningful wholes. Ruskin is on the verge of a discovery that was to have enormous consequences in the development of modern art—the realization that the work of art possesses an order peculiar to itself, obeying its own principles of unity and coherence and partaking of a reality distinct from that of nature. According to Herbert Read, Ruskin's views on the imaginative faculty amount to a precise and eloquent formulation of expressionism which applies with full force to the work of the modern Expressionists. But to regard Ruskin simply as the exponent of a full-fledged expressionist doctrine is to ignore those elements in Ruskin's make-up which withheld him from a total commitment to expressionism.

It is illuminating to consider here the views of Baudelaire, who represents a less equivocal version of expressionist aesthetics. Baudelaire's idea of the painter's imagination, essentially the same as Ruskin's, is actually the central core of his criticism, the dominant insight to which both his tastes and judgments are related. The case for imagination is based on Baudelaire's partisanship of the romantic art of Delacroix, who is actually less bold than Turner in his transformation of natural phenomena. Baudelaire connects the imaginative vision, not with truth, inner or external, but with the power "to create a suggestive magic containing at one and the same time the object and the subject, the external world and the artist himself." [17] Baudelaire's rejection of the naturalistic trends of his time, including Corot's landscapes and Courbet's realism, is a logical consequence of the expressionist position, which assigns the source of value to the subjective element in art. Despite the implications of the "Correspondences" sonnet, Baudelaire is immune to the natural religion of the English romantics and perceives its subjective character: "If an assemblage of trees, mountains, water and houses, such as we call a landscape, is beautiful, it is not so of itself, but through me, through my own grace and favour, through the idea or the feeling which I attach to it." [18] Therefore, where the claims of nature are in conflict with

those of the imagination, the latter must have priority in art.
For Delacroix the facts of nature constitute merely a point
of departure, a "dictionary." Baudelaire, of course, had not
reached the point at which he could advocate the renunciation of nature, and yet this is the ultimate logical outcome
of romantic doctrine. From the idea of the primacy of imagination proceeds the idea of its autonomy: "The artist depends on nobody but himself. He promises to the centuries
to come nothing but his own works; he guarantees nobody
but himself. He dies without children. He has been his own
king, his priest and his God." [19]

Torn between a love of nature and a love of art, Ruskin is
most indecisive concerning the individual consciousness of the
artist. Contrary to the prevailing twentieth-century preoccupation with style as the most significant element both in the
history of art and the psychology of the artist, Ruskin appears to regard it neither as a pictorial mode common to a
school of artists nor as the product of individual vision, but
as an instrumentality for recording natural facts:

What is usually called the style or manner of an artist is, in all
good art, nothing but the best means of getting at the paritcular
truth which the artist wanted; it is not a mode peculiar to himself of getting at the same truths as other men, but the *only* mode
of getting the particular facts he desires, and which mode, if
others had desired to express these facts, they also must have
adopted. All habits of execution persisted in under no such necessity, but because the artist has invented them, or desires to show
his dexterity in them, are utterly base. . . . Thus the reed pen
outline and peculiar touch of Prout which are frequently considered as mere manner, are in fact the only means of expressing
the crumbling character of stone. . . .[20]

The conception of a neutral style and the concomitant depre-
ciation of individual expression was greatly modified, however, by Ruskin's experience in Italy very soon after the
above passage was written. Under the spell of the Renais-

sance masters, his strictures against "man and his fancies, man and his trickeries, man and his inventions, poor, paltry, weak, self-sighted man" are replaced by the conception of the artist as hero. Far from being merely the intelligent observer and recorder, the authentic genius possesses transcendent powers: "To the great imaginative painter—greater a million times in every faculty of soul than we—our words may wisely be 'Come between this nature and me . . . interpret it to me; let me see with your eyes, and hear with your ears, and have help and strength from your great spirit.' " [21]

The impressionist and naturalistic aspects of Ruskin's art theory are closely allied both with romantic sensibility to nature and romantic literary theory, but are not nearly so compatible as in literary theory. Ruskin's expressionist aesthetics is not only qualified by the requirement of representational truth; it is further complicated by the semantic problem which besets expressionist theory in general: the nature and significance of that which is expressed. For Ruskin, as indeed for most later theorists of art with the exception of the strict formalists, art is a language:

Painting, or art generally, as such with all its technicalities, difficulties, and particular ends, is nothing but a noble and expressive language, invaluable as the vehicle of thought, but by itself nothing. He who has learned what is commonly considered the whole art of painting, that is, the art of representing any natural object faithfully, has as yet only learned the language by which his thoughts are to be expressed.[22]

Part of our difficulty in assessing Ruskin is one of terminology. It is not easy to supply the contemporary equivalents of the key terms in the preceding statement. By "art" he means craft or technique, but "thought" is quite ambiguous. Ruskin makes a sharper distinction between the linguistic medium and the expressive content of the arts than is allowed in modern expressionist theory. On the other hand, by subordinating the vehicle or medium of expression to that which is expressed, he tends to blur the distinction between the arts, to imply that painting exists as a vehicle for the expression of literary ideas. Although there is no equivalent in Ruskin's terminology for "form" in the current sense of the totality of visual elements by means of which the artist achieves his end, it should not be assumed that he was unaware of or indifferent to form. It is precisely the acute awareness of these visual elements which distinguishes his criticism from that of his predecessors, and he is capable of assigning to them a value greater than that of "expressiveness" or "truth." Writing of "technical composition," which approximates "form" in the current sense, he states: "It is to myself personally, the quality above others, which gives me delight in pictures. . . . Expression, sentiment, truth to nature, are essential: but all these are not enough." [23]

Ruskin's perception of the supreme importance of form remained an isolated insight which was never fully integrated into his aesthetics. Not only was it inexplicable—"the perfection of formative arrangement, as I said, cannot be explained, any more than that of melody in music" [24]—but it was beyond the powers of Ruskin's analysis. Gifted as he was in describing his own visual experiences, he was not capable of the thorough analysis of form made possible by later scholarship, principally German. And so in practice, Ruskin fell back on the description and discussion of the subject matter, that is, the literary content of pictures, rather than of their formal attributes. This is particularly true of his later criticism, which is virtually devoid of the awareness of form.

Despite its inherent contradictions, Ruskin's aesthetic theory is more acceptable to the modern reader than are his specific judgments on paintings. Similarly, his views on the ethical bearings of art are most convincing when they are most general. Although these views are voiced in theistic terms, Ruskin is now recognized as the instigator of a humanistic approach in that he attempts to relate the significance of art to the totality of human experience. Aside from the strict formalists, even his severest critics have praised this aspect of his work. Thus Geoffrey Scott, who shared virtually none of Ruskin's specific views on architecture writes:

It is fair to remember that Ruskin asserted the psychological reference of architecture. No ingenuity of technique would satisfy him, nor any abstract accuracy of scholarship . . . mere legalism, mere convention, and everything which, outside the spirit of man, might exercise lordship over the arts, he combated. No doubt his psychology was false. No doubt he utterly misinterpreted the motive of the craftsman and dogmatised too easily on the feelings of the spectator. Probably he took too slight account of the love of beauty as an emotion independent of our other desires. But still in some sense, however illusory, and by some semblance of method, however capricious, the principle was maintained: that the arts must be justified by the way they make men feel.[25]

Ruskin's psychological hypothesis is the logical outcome of his expressionistic aesthetics. But it is phrased in terms which are no longer acceptable. We tend to dismiss those pronouncements claiming a direct, causal relationship between the moral propensities of the artist and his work, ranging from the statement that the religious artist must be a saint to that which stipulates that a healthy animality is required in the greatest artists. So long as Ruskin was concerned with greatness in painting, with the relation of morality and genius, and with the tracing of causal connections between the character of a specific artist and his products, his views tend to be quite arbitrary. But in the more general area of the relation of art and society he is on much firmer ground. Although we may reject the deterministic bias of his teaching—his belief that art is an infallible index of the ethos of an age—we approve of his more general conviction that art as a human activity cannot be isolated from man's other activities, social, economic, and religious. What Ruskin perceived, almost intuitively, was the idea of cultural integration.

The development of Ruskin's thought is often explained as a progression from aesthetics to ethics to sociology. Ruskin himself denied that there was any fundamental disparity between his ideas on art and his social doctrines. Certainly in terms of feeling, all his work is invested by a single motive which is contained in the celebrated aphorism: There is no wealth but life. This slogan, the basis of Ruskin's social philosophy, may properly be construed as an aesthetic perception; it is echoed in Bernard Berenson's requirement that art be judged by the criterion of life-enhancement. Nevertheless, the shift in Ruskin's interest from landscape art and painting in general to the problem of art and society is accompanied by a modification of his aesthetic outlook. It will be noted that his most original and most important contribution to the sociology of art, the "happiness of the workman" theory has no relevance to expressionist aesthetics: "I believe the right question to ask, respecting all ornament, is simply this: Was it done with enjoyment—was the carver happy while he was about it?" [26] Ruskin did not ask this question about the possessors of imaginative vision. Indeed he is no longer concerned with greatness in art, but with the "inferior" workman: "The principal admirableness of the Gothic schools in architecture is that they thus receive the labour of inferior minds; and out of fragments full of imperfection . . . indulgently raise up a stately and unaccusable whole." [27]

Ruskin's evaluation of Gothic sculpture is based on an aesthetic judgment which has been completely reversed in our own time. He refers to the fantastic ignorance of the sculptors: "Stern statues, anatomiless and rigid; but do not mock at them, for they are signs of the life and liberty of every workman who struck the stone; a freedom of thought, and rank in scale of being, such as no laws, no charters, no chari-

ties can secure, but which it must be the first aim of all
Europe at this day to regain for her children." [28] But neither
the validity of his aesthetic judgment, nor the implied criticism of industrial society is of primary importance here. The
point is that Ruskin does not succeed in unifying the aesthetic and the ethical judgment, but deliberately subordinates
the former to the latter. One of the central doctrines of *The
Stones of Venice*—the superiority of Gothic as against the
decadence of Renaissance architecture—is not argued on aesthetic grounds: "It is not the form of this [Renaissance]
architecture against which I would plead. Its defects are
shared by many of the noblest forms of earlier building, and
might have been atoned for by the excellence of spirit. But
it is the moral nature of it which is corrupt." [29] Evidently,
so far as architecture is concerned, the ethical standard super-
sedes the aesthetic.

It would be misleading to imply that Ruskin abandoned
aesthetic criteria in his treatment of architecture, and yet in
the light of modern architecture his views must be judged
as a complete miscalculation of architectural design. He was
largely indifferent to the formal elements of buildings as
wholes; he identified architectural artistry with the decoration of the surfaces provided by the structure. The revival
of Venetian Gothic, which was the chief practical effect of
Ruskin's views on architecture, was not only aesthetically
disastrous, as he himself came to realize; his advocacy of it
represented a peculiar lapse in his judgment since it violated
his anti-academic and anti-antiquarian principles.

The principal message of *The Stones of Venice* is an aesthetic one, a restatement of the naturalism that permeates
*Modern Painters*. Ruskin considered that the prime work of
the architect was the adornment of the structure, mainly by
means of sculpture or stone carving, and that the only fit
subjects of ornament were natural objects. The shift in focus
from painting to sculpture and historically from Renaissance

and post-Renaissance art to that of the Middle Ages served
to sharpen and clarify his aesthetic outlook. While truth to
nature remains the prime criterion, the specifications of that
truth are no longer obscured by his own scientific preoccupations. The truth of art can be ascertained only by "perception and feeling, never by reasoning or report":

> Nothing must come between nature and the artist's sight; noth-
> ing between God and the artist's soul. Neither calculation nor
> hearsay . . . may be allowed to come between the universe, and
> the witness which art bears to its visible nature. The whole value
> of that witness depends on its being *eye*-witness; the whole genu-
> ineness, acceptableness, and dominion of it depend on the per-
> sonal assurance of the man who utters it.[30]

The new emphasis on immediate and personal vision and
on the emotive content of perception is remarkably prescient
of modern attitudes toward art:

> The whole function of the artist in the world is to be a seeing and
> a feeling creature; to be an instrument of such tenderness and
> sensitiveness that no shadow, no hue, no line, no instantaneous
> and evanescent expression of the visible things around him nor
> of any emotions which they are capable of conveying to the spirit
> which has been given him, shall either be left unrecorded, or fade
> from the book of record.[31]

Against the claims of science and conceptual knowledge,
Ruskin places the idea of the innocent eye or integral vision
which, whether it be psychologically valid or not, was to
play so important a part in the development of twentieth-
century art: "The whole difference between the man of
genius and other men, it has been said a thousand times and
most truly, is that the first remains in great part a child, seeing with the large eyes of children, in perpetual wonder."[32]

These theoretical pronouncements are the product of aesthetic experiences, specifically his response to the sculpture
and mosaics of St. Mark's, and the Italian primitives. In deal-

ing with works in which representation of appearances is
wholly subsidiary to expressive power, he is least equivocal
concerning the "true ends of art." He now identifies representational accuracy with the external, material content of
art and locates the "spiritual" values of art in its formal attributes:

The arrangement of colours and lines is an art analogous to the
composition of music, and entirely independent of the representation of facts. Good colouring does not necessarily convey the
image of anything but itself. It consists in certain proportions
and arrangements of rays of light, but not in likeness to anything.
. . . In like manner, as soon as a great sculptor begins to shape
his work out of the block, we shall see that its lines are nobly
arranged . . . Their likeness does not affect their nobleness.
They are magnificent forms, and that is all we need care to know
of them, in order to say whether the workman is a good or bad
sculptor.[33]

Ruskin's espousal of formalism occurs in his discussion of
naturalism as one of the elements that constitute the Gothic
style. The chapter in which it occurs, "The Nature of
Gothic," is a landmark in art criticism in that it attempts to
define style not in terms of external structural characteristics, such as the pointed arch and the groined vault, but in
those of the psychological attributes of the producers. If Ruskin was blind to the powerful rational elements of Gothic
structure, particularly as revealed in the pattern of vaulting
—art of mathematical severity—his observations on Gothic
ornament are penetrating, and his connection of its formal
elements with the mentality of the North prefigures the
method of Heinrich Wölfflin. The virtue of Gothic naturalism, according to Ruskin, resides not in its fidelity to fact,
but in its vitality and energy, qualities at once perceptible in
form and directly expressive of affective states. In effect, Ruskin adumbrates an aesthetics which links the formal order
of nature, that is, organic form, with man's emotional needs.

By suppressing the contradictions and inconsistencies, it might be possible to extract from the voluminous and tangled mass of Ruskin's works a unified theory of art which accords with modern views. It would appear that so long as he could concentrate without distraction upon actual works of art, he perceived more clearly than anyone in his time the essential nature and aims of art. But this lucidity is obscured not only by personal and private obsessions, but by a more serious blurring of focus due ultimately to his fundamental premise. The diversity of his interests and his desire to submit all of them to a universal outlook preserve his criticism from the narrowness of the specialist and from formalist solipsism; but in his effort to situate the work of art in the framework of the totality of human experience, he, and probably most of his readers, frequently lost sight of the work itself.

Ruskin's contemporary reputation did not depend, to any great extent, on his aesthetic theories, but on his stylistic gifts, his powers of persuasion; perhaps principally on the association of Ruskin the art critic and Ruskin the social prophet. It was the moral fervor of his lectures on art that had the greatest effect on the unsophisticated. His popular influence was at its height after his analytical powers had declined. Consequently, it was not his views on the imagination, on organic form, on abstraction and symbolism, but his personal predilections that formed the taste of the Victorian public. According to Joan Evans:

His influence on taste was enormous, and depended not only on his powers as a critic but also on the accidents of social history. The readers whom he most impressed by his early critical work were women of gifts and cultivation, such as Lady Canning and Lady Waterford, who set the tone for the dinner-party society of London. Their approval, coming at the time it did, carried more weight than it would have done at any other period . . . His work, in fact, was a strong staff on which the ignorant and the timid could lean in safety; his contemporary success is bound up with the rise of the wealthy manufacturing classes to a place in the social world. They needed art in an age of industrial ugliness; and they needed it with a moralistic justification. This John Ruskin provided. His want of historical background made his pronouncements yet easier of digestion by a middle-class public who shared his historical ignorance.[34]

So far as contemporary painters were concerned, Ruskin's influence was negligible. He simply ignored the tremendous activity that was taking place in France. By the time of the Whistler affair, he was incapable of a favorable response to experimental work; his standards were those of verisimilitude and congeniality of subject matter. It was his views on the art of the past that had the most salutary and most lasting effect on taste. At least two generations of English and American visitors to Italy employed his work as a guide to Italian painting. On the whole, his taste in Italian painting has stood up well to the test of time. His greatest enthusiasms—for Giotto, Botticelli, Lippi, Carpaccio, Titian, Tintoretto, and Veronese—are sound, and we can definitely ascribe to his influence the general transfer of interest from the High Renaissance to Early Renaissance, Gothic, and Romanesque work. In this respect at least Ruskin's influence extended to the more sophisticated viewer of art and even to the professional writers on art. Roger Fry's earliest work, his studies of Bellini and Giotto, belong in the tradition of art criticism established by Ruskin.

# WALTER PATER

1839  Born at Shadwell, East London, August 4. His parents,
Dr. Richard Glode Pater and Maria Hill Pater, were of
Dutch ancestry. Jean Baptiste Pater, the French painter,
is believed to be of the same stock. Pater's father, a surgeon,
left the Catholic church before his marriage, but adopted
no other formal faith. His children were brought up in the
Anglican church. After the early death of his father, Pater
lived with his mother and grandmother in Enfield, where
he was privately tutored by the headmaster of Enfield
Grammar School. Two of Pater's Imaginary Portraits,
"The Child in the House" and "Emerald Uthwart," are
fictional accounts of his childhood.

1853  Entered King's School, Canterbury, his mother having
moved to Harbledown in order to make his attendance
possible. He appeared to be happy at school, despite his indifference to sports and games. A serious, meditative boy,
he was already destined for the contemplative life. His
mother's death occurred shortly after he returned to school
for his second year. A year later he met John Keble at
Hursley, who strengthened his determination to choose a
religious vocation. During this period, he wrote poetry,
most of which has not survived. In his last year at school
he read Ruskin's *Modern Painters,* which revealed to him
the world of art.

1858 Entered Queen's College, Oxford. Though interested in
logic and metaphysics, he devoted most of his time to classical studies. He attracted the notice of Benjamin Jowett,
the most eminent classical scholar of his time. During his
first two years at college he spent his vacation with his
sisters in Heidelberg and Dresden. During this period his
religious beliefs were undermined by his reading in philosophy. He continued to attend Anglican services, however, during his lifetime.

1862 Took his degree, a second-class in *Literae Humaniores*.
His wish to be ordained in the Church of England was
frustrated by the intervention of two college friends, who
opposed him on the grounds of his skepticism.

1863 Elected member of Old Mortality, an Oxford essay society.
His efforts to obtain a fellowship, first at Trinity College,
Oxford, and then at Brasenose, were unsuccessful.

1864 Was granted a probationary, nonclerical fellowship at
Brasenose on the basis of his knowledge of German philosophy.

1865 Became an actual fellow of Brasenose. Toured Italy with
his pupil, C. L. Shadwell, later his literary executor. This
trip served to intensify Pater's enthusiasm for the art of
the Renaissance, which was eventually to become one of
his chief interests.

1866– Published an essay on Winckelmann in the *Westminster*
1873 *Review* (1866); essays on Leonardo da Vinci, Botticelli,
Pico della Mirandola, and Michelangelo appeared in the
*Fortnightly Review* (1869–1871). These essays, amplified
by several others, a Preface, and a Conclusion, formed his
first book, *Studies in the History of the Renaissance* (1873),
which established Pater's reputation as a critic and aesthete.
This book brought him many admirers, the most vocal of
whom was Oscar Wilde.

1874 Hoped to receive the proctorship at the disposal of Brasenose, but was opposed by Benjamin Jowett, who disapproved of *The Renaissance*. Published essays on Wordsworth and *Measure for Measure* in the *Fortnightly Review*.

1875– Led a quiet, sequestered existence at Oxford. Made few
1880 intimate friends. Continued to spend his long vacations on the Continent, chiefly in France and Italy. During this period he was absorbed in Greek studies. "Demeter and Persephone" and "A Study of Dionysus" appeared in the *Fortnightly Review*. "The Child in the House," an autobiographical sketch, appeared in *Macmillan's Magazine* (1878).

1880 Resigned toutorship at Brasenose in order to devote his full time to writing.

1882 Spent the winter in Rome, working on *Marius the Epicurean,* a philosophical novel on which he had been engaged since 1878.

1885– *Marius the Epicurean* was published in two volumes (1885).
1889 Pater moved to London, where he remained for eight years, although he retained his Brasenose address during the school terms. Continued to visit France and Italy with his sisters for several weeks each year. Began contributing reviews to the *Guardian,* the *Pall-Mall Gazette,* and the *Athenaeum*. Several of his Imaginary Portraits appeared in literary journals. *The Renaissance* went into a third edition (1888) with the Conclusion restored; it had been suppressed by Pater in the second edition, on the grounds that it might be misinterpreted by the young.

1890 Delivered a lecture on Prosper Mérimée in Oxford before a large audience which was an indication of Pater's growing reputation.

1891  Began work on *Plato and Platonism,* based on university lectures, his last major composition. It was published two years later and received Jowett's approbation.

1893  Moved from London to St. Giles, Oxford.

1894  Received an honorary LL.D. from the University of Glasgow. Died suddenly on July 30.


WALTER PATER is not usually bracketed with the art critics. We think of him primarily as a man of letters—the master of an exquisite, though excessively labored style—who incidentally possessed a taste for the visual arts. Even as a literary man, he casts a vague image, his criticism verging on poetic creation, his fiction tending toward the reflective, philosophical essay. The image is persistent, however, and has survived nearly a half-century of neglect. It is best defined in Iain Fletcher's brief but excellent monograph:

He remains the classic example of a type of temperament in whom we can recognize certain subdued and almost inexpressible moments of the self, its moments of wistfulness and hesitation and its partial triumphs of perception; and more than Marius, or any of those shadowy half-created characters in the *Imaginary Portraits,* he has created himself for us in his *oeuvre* as a permanently significant symbolical figure: the most complete example, the least trivial, of the aesthetic man.[1]

Pater's essays on Renaissance art and Greek sculpture are no longer seriously regarded as a reliable source either of historical information or aesthetic enlightenment, and yet there were innumerable young men in the last century and the early part of this whose interest in the visual arts was first aroused by reading them. For Oscar Wilde, *The Renaissance* was "my golden book," and Arthur Symons, William Sharp, Lionel Johnson, and William Butler Yeats regarded him as master. Bernard Berenson acknowledged his debt to Pater as his first mentor on early Florentine and Venetian art, but long after he had outstripped Pater in knowledge of painting he continued to accept *Marius* as a guide to the art of life— "the art, namely, of so reliving the ideal or poetic traits, the elements of distinction in our everyday life . . . that the un- adorned remainder of it, the mere drift and debris of our days, comes to be as though it were not." [2]

Although Pater's writings on art do not rank with Ruskin's work as a major contribution to aesthetics or art criticism, they served to crystallize and make explicit an outlook only latent in Ruskin—the conviction that art represents the high- est value in existence—which, once its full implications be- came clear, was repugnant to Ruskin. Having awakened his audience to the full imaginative and emotional potential of the visual arts, Ruskin was the involuntary progenitor of the aestheticism with which the name of Pater is associated. The phrase "art for art's sake" is highly ambiguous; in the con- text of literary criticism it has acquired an almost totally pejorative connotation. Applied to Pater, it has a double sense. If it refers to aestheticism as a theory of the conduct of life, a mode of achieving perfection of the self by means of a balance of culture and feeling, it should be interpreted as meaning art for the sake of a highly specialized morality. In the narrower context of aesthetics, insofar as it specifies the ontology of art, art for art's sake has a certain validity on purely empirical grounds, since the central fact concerning modern art is the assumption, whether overt or concealed, that the work of art requires no justification other than its own existence. As a critical doctrine, art for art's sake implies that the work of art be apprehended and judged on its own terms rather than by extrinsic standards.

It is unfair to saddle Pater with responsibility for the excesses of art for art's sake, specifically with the advocacy of a complete divorce of art and life. In the essay on "Style" (1888), he himself reverted to the traditional view that the judgment of the literary work must ultimately be a moral judgment transcending aesthetic criteria. Actually the Preface and Conclusion to *The Renaissance* (1873), upon which Pater's fame as an aesthete was based, do not stipulate the autonomy of the work of art. The Preface, an exposition of critical method, deliberately renounces concern with fundamental aesthetic questions, with the nature and function of art:

> In aesthetic criticism the first step towards seeing one's object as it really is, is to know one's own impression as it really is, to discriminate it, to realize it distinctly . . . he who experiences these impressions strongly . . . has no need to trouble himself with the abstract question what beauty is in itself, or what its exact relation to truth or experiences—metaphysical questions, as unprofitable as metaphysical questions elsewhere.[3]

The Conclusion has even less to say concerning aesthetics; in it Pater placed aesthetics within the sphere of ethics, exhorting the reader to pursue a way of life in which aesthetic experience has the highest value, but making no specifications concerning the nature of that experience.

Although the Preface and Conclusion do not formally commit Pater to art for art's sake, he cannot be exonerated from a charge of aestheticism. There is little doubt that he was predisposed to it by temperament and background. One cannot help feeling, furthermore, that the tone of the essays which constitute the body of *The Renaissance* was to some extent determined by Ruskin's presence at Oxford as Slade Professor. Whatever subtlety Ruskin's views on the relation of art to morality may have once possessed, it was no longer in evidence in his Oxford lectures; Ruskin's heavy-handed moralizing may well have provoked an extreme reaction in

Pater. Quite apart from the explicit repudiation of moral judgment, there is another circumstance which tended to confirm the aestheticism of *The Renaissance*. The original title, *Studies in the History of the Renaissance,* led a contemporary reviewer, Mrs. Mark Pattison, to complain that the work failed to point out the vital relationships between Renaissance art and the main movements—social, political, and intellectual—of the period. Although it was not Pater's intention to write either a history of the Renaissance or a history of Renaissance art, the critique does point to a serious shortcoming in his critical procedure. Just as his critical theory dispenses with philosophical knowledge, his art criticism makes little use of his extensive historical culture. He disavows interest in "periods, types, schools of taste," preferring to locate the specific virtue of the work of art in its direct commerce with the sensibility of the spectator. He makes a broad generalization to the effect that fifteenth-century Italian art owes its specific quality to an "intimate alliance with mind, participation in the best thoughts which the age produced," but in the essays devoted to the Renaissance painters, he links the specific aesthetic virtue to the personality of the artist rather than to the age in which he lived.

Although Pater manifested little or no interest in social and political questions, historical or contemporary, it would be unfair to tax him with an indifference to ideas, but it must be admitted that for him even ideas possess a quasi-aesthetic quality. He is inclined to savor the temper of a philosopher or the intellectual tone of a religious system as he would a work of art. Pater's reserve and decorum strike us as being infinitely more civilized than Ruskin's inspired though manic preaching, his relativism and skepticism more congenial to our age than Ruskin's dogmatism. But even if aesthetic experience is the highest form of experience for Pater, he fails to give a sense of the importance of art which Ruskin conveys. The reason for this lies, I think, in the fact that Pater is too much concerned with the spectator's role in the aesthetic transaction, the heightened intensity of the viewer's experience, rather than with the life and intensity inherent in the work itself.

To some extent this deficiency resulted from Pater's lack of technical knowledge, which deprived him of the means for designating the specifically formal elements which are the proper subject of aesthetic criticism. Pater eventually recognized the need for a technical, formalist approach, but in the Preface to *The Renaissance* "aesthetic criticism" signifies impressionistic criticism. The role of the amateur, more evident in his writings on art than in his literary criticism, precluded his sharing, even imaginatively, in the creative act. The word "passion," which occurs frequently in Pater's account of aesthetic experience, refers to the spectator's response to the work rather than to the artist's attitude. Pater's real gift is for the discernment of the delicate nuance rather than of power; he is more successful in dealing with Luca della Robbia than with Michelangelo. By taste and temperament he was inclined toward refinement rather than robustness, toward the contemplative rather than the dramatic. Unfortunately, Pater's personal predilections were confused with his aesthetic theories; the penchant for decadence, more discernible in *The Renaissance* than in his later work, was readily assimilable with the atmosphere of the Aesthetic Movement of the eighties and nineties. Pater, more than most literary figures, has suffered from the excesses of his followers. The irony lies in the fact that the aura of abandon should have lent itself to one whose personal life was so circumspect, so retiring.

The cloistered quality of Pater's existence is, unfortunately, communicated to his writings on art, and vitiates his work to some extent. Both art and literature were sometimes regarded by him as mere appurtenances of culture:

Different classes of persons at different times, make, of course, very various demands upon literature. Still, scholars, I suppose, and not only scholars, but all disinterested lovers of books, will always look to it, as to all other fine art, for a refuge, a sort of cloistral refuge, from a certain vulgarity in the actual world. A perfect poem like *Lycidas,* a perfect fiction like *Esmond,* the perfect handling of a theory like Newman's *Idea of a University,* has for them something of the use of a religious "retreat." [4]

This attitude has been used against Pater as a warrant of his incompetence, his refusal to deal with literature as an embodiment of reality. Perhaps this attitude is not so offensive with respect to the visual arts, where realism, though it has its adherents, is no longer the leading cry.

The effect of Pater's dilettantism might have been mitigated had he chosen to deal with contemporary art as well as with the art of antiquity and the Renaissance. Pater makes glancing references to contemporary artists, to Ingres and Legros among others, which indicate a receptivity to the art of his time. His review of George Moore's *Modern Painting* reveals an open mind toward the French Impressionists, if not an actual knowledge of their work. But in the main his all-absorbing interest was in art remote from his own time, and hence from the "actual world." Purged of its associations with decadence and escapism, Pater's point of view emphasizes the significant contemplative element in aesthetic experience, which had been clearly recognized in the eighteenth century but tended to be slighted in the more pragmatic atmosphere of his time, as it is in ours. At any rate, Pater did not share the current view that the hedonistic aspects of aesthetic experience somehow detract from the dignity and significance of art.

I have noted as one of Ruskin's critical shortcomings his tendency to concern himself with matters that are involved in the genesis of the work but not actually visible or demon-

strable in the work. If, according to an influential segment
of current critical doctrine, aesthetic criticism is "intrinsic,"
that is, addresses itself to the concrete phenomena embodied
in the work itself, Ruskin is guilty of the "genetic fallacy,"
as are all critics who devote themselves to the psychology of
the artist or to his social milieu. Inasmuch as Pater's studies
are an inquiry into the personalities of the Renaissance painters, he is also culpable. His essay on Leonardo da Vinci
centers on the "mystery in his work, and something enigmat-
ical beyond the usual measure of great men." Pater's procedure seems very odd in an age familiar with a psychological approach to art: "A lover of strange souls may still analyse
for himself the impression made on him by those works, and
try to reach through it a definition of the chief elements of
Leonardo's genius." [5] Pater proposes an analysis, not of the
works, but of his subjective impressions of them. In terms of
the intrinsic approach, this constitutes the affective fallacy
in criticism.

The most flagrant example of the affective fallacy in
Pater is his description of "La Gioconda," the climax of his
essay on Leonardo and probably the most famous piece of
art criticism in English, though it is an early work (1869)
and not truly representative of Pater's critical abilities. After
the statement concerning the "unfathomable smile, always
with a touch of something sinister in it" the palpable work
is abandoned for a purely lyric flight, a prose poem bearing
only a most tenuous relationship to its subject:

The presence, that thus rose as strangely beside the waters, is
expressive of what in the ways of a thousand years men had come
to desire . . . She is older than the rocks among which she sits;
like a vampire, she has been dead many times, and learned the
secrets of the grave . . . and all this has been to her but as the
sound of lyres and flutes . . . The fancy of a perpetual life,
sweeping together ten thousand experiences is an old one; and
modern thought has conceived the idea of humanity as wrought

upon by and summing up in itself all modes of thought and life. Certainly Lady Lisa might stand as the embodiment of the old fancy, the symbol of the modern idea.[6]

The extraordinary success of the passage suggests that it manages, perhaps by means of prose cadence and imagery, to express more than a subjective impression, that is, to capture some quality inherent in the picture. One cavils only at its inclusion within the category of criticism, even of impressionist criticism.

The critical program announced in the Preface to *The Renaissance,* though frankly and necessarily subjective, does not give license for wayward flights of fancy. "To know one's own impression as it really is, to discriminate it, to realise it distinctly" would appear to be indispensable conditions of a valid criticism of the visual arts, inasmuch as the object must be apprehended by means of sense impressions. To know one's own impression is equivalent to the act of seeing. From the point of view of the twentieth-century formalists, the further requirements, those of discriminating and realizing the visual impression, would nearly exhaust the critic's functions. The formalist critic does not rely on pure sensibility, of course, but on a sensibility operating through some visual system or scheme by means of which he can describe, analyze, and interpret sense impressions. Pater, as I have already noted, did not possess the technical knowledge necessary for the formulation of such a system. His art criticism is therefore limited by his equipment for verbalizing the product of a refined and acute visual sensibility—that of a literary man. Inasmuch as it was a translation of pictorial elements in literary terms, Pater's critical practice, with a few exceptions to be noted, violated the formalists' prohibition of "literary" interpretation. Yet the theory, particularly the theory of pictorial form he outlined in "The School of Giorgione," is an important document in formalist criticism. Ruskin possessed the technical information and the capacity for describing art in visual terms which are required in formalist criticism, but the formalists denied the relevance of the ethical and social content of his criticism to aesthetics.

Without speculating on the autonomous character of aesthetic experience, Pater attempted to view the work of art as it really is, disencumbered of extrinsic considerations:

The aesthetic critic, then, regards all the objects with which he has to do, all works of art, and the fairer forms of nature and human life, as powers or forces producing pleasurable sensations, each of a more or less peculiar and unique kind . . . And the function of the aesthetic critic is to distinguish, analyze, and separate from its adjuncts, the virtue by which a picture, a landscape, a fair personality in life or in a book, produces this special impression of beauty or pleasure, to indicate what the source of that impression is, and under what conditions it is experienced. His end is reached when he has disengaged that virtue and noted it, as a chemist notes some natural element, for himself and others. . . . What is important, then, is not that the critic should possess a correct abstract definition of beauty for the intellect, but a certain kind of temperament, the power of being deeply moved by the presence of beautiful objects.[7]

Although it obviates such distractions to aesthetic criticism as social and ethical matters and even aesthetic preconceptions, the critical procedure outlined here surrenders too readily the possibility of objectivity, "to see the object as it really is." Later formalist critical theory concedes the inevitability of personal predilection in aesthetic emotion, but holds out the promise of formal analysis which minimizes subjective preferences. The essays on Leonardo, Botticelli, and Michelangelo are primarily studies of personality as reflected in works of art. It is not Pater's inclination to locate the source of the specific aesthetic "virtue" of an artist's work in his personality, nor the fact that he is drawn toward certain artists by temperamental affinity, that is at fault, but his tendency to identify himself with his subjects, to view them as exensions of his own personality. Pater did eventually hit upon a literary form, the imaginary portrait, which suited his gifts more perfectly than the critical essay.

Although Pater's reputation is that of an aesthete—one whose sensibilities are highly developed and who devotes his life to their cultivation—his ultimate concern was ethical, growing out of his personal predicament with respect to the religious crisis of his age. Ruskin's most vigorous writing on art coincided with the period of his most ardent religious faith. And although that faith was subject to several transformations during his lifetime, his constant practice was to subsume his aesthetics under a theistic outlook. For Pater the subordination of aesthetic emotion to religious feeling was no longer possible. As T. S. Eliot observed in his essay on Pater, the effect of his writings was to extend to the field of art Matthew Arnold's concept of culture as a substitute for religion. Whether or not Eliot's contention ignores the authenticity of religious feeling in *Marius the Epicurean,* it is borne out by the Conclusion to *The Renaissance.* The argument of the Conclusion issues from a virtually total religious skepticism. Human knowledge is reduced to the operations of the universe of matter. From an atomistic hypothesis of flux, change, and impermanence is deduced the inexorable isolation of the individual consciousness—the thick wall of personality. It should be noted that Pater's sense of isolation was deeply rooted in his temperament, and that the philosophical hypothesis, though sincere, is probably the rationalization of a serious emotional lack on Pater's part, revealed by his incapacity after childhood to experience an intimate relationship.

The exhortation to burn with a "hard gem-like flame" follows from the philosophical premise. From the phenomenalism of modern science, which reduces experience to a series of discrete sensations, Pater argues that true economy in the ethical sense calls for the greatest possible cultivation of sensuous awareness. The emphasis is on quantity as well as on quality of aesthetic experience, on its intensity and variety:

Only be sure it is passion—that it does yield you this fruit of a quickened, multiplied consciousness. Of this wisdom, the poetic passion, the desire of beauty, the love of art for art's sake, has most; for art comes to you professing frankly to give nothing but the highest quality to your moments as they pass, and simply for these moments' sake.[8]

In this context, "art for art's sake" has little or no critical relevance. It refers neither to the internal constitution of the work of art, nor to its production. Applied to the practitioner, the "religion of art"—the justification of the superiority of art to all other experience and hence of a life devoted exclusively to art—has a certain ethical validity. It was the creed, moreover, which was adopted almost wholesale by the most genuinely creative visual artists of the past century. But the doctrine of art for art's sake adumbrated in the Conclusion is mainly concerned with the appreciation of art. The great deficiency of Pater's writing on art, so evident in contrast with Ruskin, is its emphasis on receptivity, on the passive response of art. This aspect of Pater's art criticism is intensified by his almost exclusive concern with the firmly established art of the past. In theory at least, Pater's attitude encouraged receptivity to the new and experimental, as the following indicates:

For us the Renaissance is the name of a many-sided but yet united movement, in which the love of the things of the intellect and the imagination for their own sake, the desire for a more liberal and comely way of concerning life, make themselves felt, urging those who experience this desire to search out first one and then another means of intellectual and imaginative enjoyment, and directing them not merely to the discovery of old and forgotten sources of this enjoyment, but to divine new sources of it, new experiences, new subjects of poetry, new forms of art.[9]

Pater's relativism and his strictures against the formation of habit should have reinforced this attitude. Herbert Read, for one, believes that Pater would have welcomed the radical art of the twentieth century—Proust and Kafka, Bartok and Stravinsky, Picasso and Henry Moore. Yet while there is no definite evidence to disprove Read's contention, one nevertheless senses in Pater a nostalgia for the past more pervasive than a sympathy for contemporary work.

Whereas Ruskin was drawn to early Renaissance and Gothic art, Pater's tastes are more conventional. He is attracted mainly to classical art, to Greek sculpture, and to the classical element in Renaissance art. He manages to work into his Renaissance studies an essay on Winckelmann, the great eighteenth-century German art historian, a figure with whom Pater cannot help identifying himself. What appeals to Pater in both the personality and work of Winckelmann is the frank affirmation of the pagan outlook, the affirmation of the sensuous element in the life of the imagination:

Winckelmann here reproduces for us the earlier sentiment of the Renaissance. On a sudden the imagination feels itself free. How facile and direct, it seems to say, is this life of the senses and the understanding, when once we have apprehended it! Here, surely, is the more liberal life we have been seeking so long . . . How mistaken and roundabout have been our effort to reach it by mystic passion and monastic reverie; how they have deflowered the flesh; how little they have emancipated us.[10]

The classical tradition in the visual arts represented for Pater as it did for Winckelmann the norm by which all subsequent art is to be measured and according to which nearly all other art is in a sense and a degree decadent: "The longer we contemplate that Hellenic ideal, in which man is at unity with himself, with his physical nature, with the outward world, the more we may be inclined to regret that he should ever have passed beyond it, to contend for a perfection that makes the blood turbid, and frets the flesh, and discredits the actual world about us. . . ."[11] Although Pater shares Winckelmann's nostalgia for a "golden age" of art, represented by what both of them conceived to be the greatest period of Greek sculpture—that of the fifth century—he adopts a more "advanced" point of view in deprecating Winckelmann's inability to appreciate nonclassical art—"the subtle and penetrative, but somewhat grotesque art of the modern world." In spite of his admiration for the pagan ideal, frankly sensual and unclouded by doubt, conflict, and melancholy, Pater's real affinity was precisely for that aspect of Renaissance art in which the Hellenistic element is in conflict with the Christian. The charm of Leonardo, Michelangelo, and Botticelli for him lies in a certain mysterious, ambiguous, and, we might say, "decadent" quality. Here, perhaps, Pater is too prone to romanticize the Renaissance, to read into it the dichotomies of his own state of mind. He discerns the specific aesthetic quality or "virtue" of Leonardo's art to be its modernity, the intrusion of spirit into the classic world of sense:

Sometimes this curiosity came into conflict with the desire of beauty; it tended to make him go too far below that outside of things in which art begins and ends. The struggle between the reason and its ideas, and the senses, the desire of beauty is the key to Leonardo's life at Milan . . . Now he was to entertain in this narrow medium those divinations of a humanity too wide for it, that larger vision of the opening world, which is not only too much for the great irregular art of Shakespeare.[12]

Botticelli also, in Pater's angle of vision, is an artist torn between two world-views, between the simplicities of religion and naturalism and a "modern" introspection and subtlety. From this conflict arises "the peculiar sentiment with which he infuses his profane and sacred persons, comely, and in a certain sense like angels, but with a sense of displacement or loss about them—the wistfulness of exiles, conscious of a passion and energy greater than any known issue of them explains, which runs through all his varied work with a sentiment of ineffable melancholy." [13]

It is evident from these passages, as it is from all the central essays on the visual arts including "The School of Giorgione," which postulates a conception of pictorial form as independent of subject matter, that Pater is concerned primarily with representational elements. In this respect, there is no radical difference between the aesthetic outlook of Ruskin and Pater. Nor is there a great divergence in matters of taste. Although Pater exhibits a predilection for the morbid and decadent, his preferences, so far as period is concerned, are more conventional than Ruskin's. The contrast in their personalities could hardly be greater, and yet it is fairly clear that Pater's visual response to painting was determined by Ruskin. One concludes that, despite a fundamental disagreement concerning the ethical import of art, Pater's art criticism is a direct continuation of Ruskin's. Yet Pater maintains a curious silence about Ruskin's influence—indeed, about Ruskin's existence. The only recorded reference betrays a sharp note of rivalry, even of hostility; "A friend remembers that he [Pater] was once talking of the artistic perceptions of Ruskin, and said suddenly with a show of impatience, 'I cannot believe that Ruskin saw more in the church of St. Mark than I do.' " [14] Pater's biographer reveals what one had already suspected, that the only definite artistic influence was that of Ruskin, whom Pater had read at the age of nineteen.

It would be absurd to imply that before Ruskin, cultured Englishmen had been completely insensitive to the visual arts. What Ruskin perceived and what Pater learned from him was that the real significance of the visual arts derived neither from technical skill in representation nor from the grandeur of the subject matter but from the capacity to convey emotion by means of an imaginative transformation of the data of visual appearances. Pater's hedonism, it is hardly necessary to explain, does not counsel submission to undefined sensuous experience, but to the life of the senses transformed into art by what Pater called "imaginative reason." Despite his revolt against a puritanical culture, which took the form of nostalgia for an uninhibited paganism, he valued a work of art primarily as an expression of the human spirit, embracing emotion, intellect, and imagination.

The precursor of both Ruskin's and Pater's aesthetic views was the romantic doctrine of imagination. The romantic strain in Ruskin's art theory was strongly conditioned, as I have already observed, by a religious dogma which imposed certain limits on the scope of the visual arts, principally the requirement of naturalism, the definition of which varied considerably in his work, but otherwise remained constant. It should also be remembered that Ruskin's social theories were motivated by religious conviction and that his social interests tended to modify his theory of art. Pater, on the other hand, represents a secular version of the romantic theory of art; he is much closer than Ruskin to Baudelaire and the Symbolists on the question of naturalism. Pater is relatively cautious concerning the prerogative of the artist to transform natural facts in the interests of imaginative vision. He does not actually go as far as Whistler in this respect. It is his attitude toward the relationship of art and nature which constitutes his divergence from Ruskin. For Ruskin art is subordinate to nature and is to be judged by its conformity to what he conceived of as natural laws. Pater, on the other hand, was inclined to view nature through the medium of art. The role of nature in art does not figure in his aesthetic doctrine; his attitude can be deduced from his aesthetic interests:

. . . nature is to him always a setting, a background, subordinated to the human interest . . . The home, the house, the room, the furniture and decoration, the garden . . . , all these were nearer to his heart than nature in her wilder and sterner aspects, because the thought and hand of humanity had passed over them, writing its care and its dreams legibly on cornice and lintel, on panel and beam, on chest and press, on alley and bower, on border and fountain.[15]

Although Pater's interest in the art of the human figure was far greater than in landscape, here also he was not at all concerned with the problem of representational accuracy. The idealized human figure of classical sculpture constituted for him the norm of beauty as it had done for eighteenth-century art criticism. He is not, therefore, committed to a canon of realism and recognizes deviations from it as an expressive device. The discussion of Renaissance sculpture in "Luca della Robbia" points, in a most tentative manner, toward the notion of abstract art. Pater is speaking of the special limitation of sculpture which results from the material conditions of the medium, tending toward a hard realism verging on caricature: "Against this tendency to the hard presentment of mere form trying vainly to compete with the reality of nature itself, all noble sculpture constantly struggles; each great system of sculpture resisting it in its own way, etherealizing, spiritualizing, relieving its hardness, its heaviness, and death." [16] The terminology is highly reminiscent of Ruskin, and indeed there is no basic discrepancy between Ruskin's and Pater's attitude toward realism insofar as they both subscribe to the central tenet of romantic expressionist theory—that the main business of art is not the imitation of objective reality but the projection of an inner vision or emotion.

Ruskin, of course, did not completely resolve the tension between expressionism and the mimetic doctrine imposed by his theology. The role of nature is less ambiguous in Ruskin's aesthetics than in his art criticism. According to *Modern Painters,* volume II, beauty is an objective phenomenon independent of the beholder, existing in the forms of nature, which can be arranged in a hierarchy headed by organic forms. The beauty of a work of art is therefore derivative, depending on a correspondence with natural forms. While Ruskin fully recognizes the function of the imagination in art, he attributes to it an intuitive grasp of natural forms. Now Pater is noncommittal in the realm of aesthetics:

> Beauty, like all other qualities presented to human experience, is relative; and the definition of it becomes unmeaning and useless in proportion to its abstractness. To define beauty, not in the most abstract, but in the most concrete terms possible, to find not a universal formula for it, but the formula which expresses most adequately this or that special manifestation of it, is the aim of the true student of aesthetics.[17]

Pater's relativism is not so thorough-going in practice as in theory; he consistently associates artistic excellence with "strangeness." This might be ascribed simply to a preference for the exotic—a variant of the romantic love of the remote and the irregular, except that Pater converts it into an aesthetic principle:

> A certain strangeness, something of the blossoming of the aloe, is indeed an element in all true works of art; that they shall excite and surprise us is indispensable. But that they shall give pleasure and exert a charm over us is indispensable too; and this strangeness must be sweet also—a lovely strangeness. . . .[18]

The strangeness so highly valued by Pater is closely related to the expressive element, that inward vision or emotion which is objectified in the work of art. Pater undoubtedly owes this aspect of his critical theory to the romantic movement in literature of which he is an heir. His distinction lies in his peculiar susceptibility to expressive elements in the visual arts. The passage on strangeness, which occurs in the essay on Michelangelo, may be elucidated and amplified by another reference to the same artist:

When Michelangelo came, with a genius spiritualized by the reverie of the middle age, penetrated by its spirit of inwardness and introspection, living not a mere outward life like the Greek, but a life full of inward experiences, sorrows, consolations, a system which sacrificed so much of what was inward and unseen could not satisfy him. To him, lover and student of Greek sculpture as he was, work which did not bring what was inward to the surface, which was not concerned with individual expression, with individual character and feeling, the special history of the special soul was not worth doing at all . . . he secured for his work individuality and intensity of expression, while he avoided a too hard realism, that tendency to harden into caricature which the representation of feeling must always have.[19]

The reference to caricature shows Pater's tendency to associate expressiveness in the visual arts with facial expression. While his reaction to the enigmatic smile of "Mona Lisa" or the peevish-looking Madonnas of Botticelli are memorable, his concept of expressiveness is not confined to the literary, anecdotal, or psychological content of painting. Michelangelo's expressiveness is explained in formal terms. The rough texture of his sculpture which is actually perfect finish, the apparent incompleteness of nearly all of it, has an effect comparable to that of time and accident on certain classical works, and is actually a technical equivalent of color, a means of imparting vitality to the hardness of the medium. Thus by a deliberate formal device the artist achieves what Pater calls spirituality.

Even in his early essays on art Pater was not given to assigning the significance of a work to its literary or anecdotal subject matter—the paramount offense in art criticism according to the current view, upon which formalism has left its mark even when it is no longer regarded as an adequate basis for a total account of art. In distinguishing between Botticelli's treatment of religious subjects and the simple naturalism of his predecessors, he notes that the real matter of Botticelli is not the iconographic content, which is merely the ostensible subject, but the undercurrent of feeling portrayed. Although his observations on Renaissance sculputre appear to prefigure a formal approach which was more clearly defined in his later work, he is still primarily concerned with those elements of expression which could be apprehended in psychological rather than formal terms. The significant duality at this point was feeling vs. subject matter rather than form vs. content.

The transition to a full-fledged formalism can be discerned in the essay on "Style." It is significant that here Pater is dealing with literary style, a topic on which he possessed the kind of expert knowledge which he lacked in the field of visual art. In designating style as an aesthetic differentia, perhaps the most essential, since of all aesthetic elements it is most intimately connected with personality, Pater invokes the term "truth," which is omnipresent in Ruskin but which Pater had hitherto scrupulously avoided. Pater is discussing the difference between communicative and imaginative discourse. He concedes to the former a modest aesthetic function, and along with it a limited merit to the truth to fact which occupies so prominent a place in Ruskin's art theory:

For just in proportion as the writer's aim, consciously or unconsciously, comes to be the transcribing, not of the world, not of mere fact, but of his sense of it, he becomes an artist, his work *fine* art; and good art (as I hope ultimately to show) in proportion to the truth of his presentment of that sense; as in those humbler or plainer functions of literature also, truth—truth to bare fact, there—is the essence of such artistic quality as they may have. Truth! there can be no merit, no craft at all without that. And further, all beauty is in the long run only fineness of truth, or what we call expression, the finer accommodation of speech

to that vision within . . . Literary art, that is, like all art which
is in any way imitative or reproductive of fact—form, or colour,
or incident—is the representation of such fact as connected with
soul, of a specific personality, in its preference, its volition and
power. Such is the matter of imaginative or artistic literature.[20]

Without actually renouncing the mimetic or representational function of art, Pater unequivocally subordinates it to
expression, regarded as the specifically aesthetic attribute;
furthermore, by identifying expression with style, the emphasis is placed on the formal element, or perhaps more accurately, on the indissoluble bond between form and subject
matter. Pater guards against the assumption that style is a
superficial or adventitious quality of the work of art. For,
if it is the product of subjective emotion or vision, it is not
dependent on the caprice of the individual artist and therefore to be regarded as mere mannerism; the stipulation of
truth guarantees its authenticity. Pater's proposition concerning the inner necessity, the inevitability, of style is demonstrated by an examination of Flaubert's idea of *le mot juste,*
one of the salient examples of the aesthetic approach to literary art. Pater's version of expressionism, based on an absolute correspondence between the aesthetic element and the
vision within, bears a certain resemblance to Benedetto
Croce's identification of expression and intuition. Yet Pater,
for all his fascination with the manifestations of personality
in the work of the Renaissance painters, is too deeply committed to the classical tradition which stresses structure and
volition—"which forsees the end in the beginning and never
loses sight of it"—to subscribe fully either to an intuitive or
a transcendental theory of art. He rejects Coleridge's idea of
the imagination, which for modern critics is the central statement of romantic aesthetics:

What makes his view a one-sided one is, that in it the artist has
become almost a mechanical agent; instead of the most luminous
and self-possessed phase of consciousness, the associative act in

art or poetry is made to look like some blindly organic process of assimilation. The work of art is likened to a living organism. That expresses truly the sense of a self-delighting, independent life which the finished work of art gives us; it hardly figures the process by which such a work was produced . . . The philosophic critic, at least, will value, even in works of imagination, seemingly the most intuitive, the power of understanding in them, their logical processes of construction, the spectacle of supreme intellectual dexterity which they afford.[21]

The traditionalism of the essay on "Style" is most pronounced in its final paragraphs, in which Pater makes amends for the aestheticism which had outraged many of his contemporaries. Here he limits the capacities of aesthetic criticism to a primary stage in the whole critical process, which is completed by an ethical judgment. This act of recantation is not necessarily to be viewed as concession to his detractors nor as a renunciation of his former views, since it largely exempts the nonliterary arts:

The distinction between great art and good art depending immediately, as regards literature at all events, not on its form, but on the matter . . . It is on the quality of the matter it informs or controls, its compass, its variety, its allegiance to great ends, or the depth of the note of revolt, or the largeness of hope in it, that the greatness of literary art depends.[22]

The essay on "Style" represents a significant alteration in Pater's critical theory from the overstated impressionism of the Preface—a prime example of the "affective fallacy"—toward the "intrinsic" approach, which in our own time places high value on stylistic analysis. Had Pater been able to apply the insights of this essay to the visual arts, his stature as an art critic would have been immeasurably increased. Ideally, Pater should have developed the principal idea of "The School of Giorgione" concerning the importance of medium in determining the formal constitution of the work of art into a conception of pictorial style, in which the formal elements are seen as the embodiment of the painter's inner vision. But to perceive Giorgione's achievement in terms of style would have required the kind of connoisseurship and technical and historical knowledge that Pater simply did not possess. He would have had to place Giorgione's individual style in relation to the Venetian school in particular, to Italian Renaissance painting in general, and ultimately to the whole history of art conceived of in terms of the evaluation and transmission of styles.

Nevertheless "The School of Giorgione," as far as it goes, is a notable document in art criticism, providing the rationale, if not the means, for the formal analysis of style. It is a carefully reasoned work, the major part of which is devoted to relatively abstract critical theory, and not at all characteristic of the impressionist approach announced in the Preface. Pater begins in the vein of Lessing's *Laocöon* by enforcing the distinction between the visual arts and literature and by protesting the traditional kind of literary treatment of painting. Unlike Lessing, who makes the mimetic capability the distinguishing factor, Pater concentrates on the sensuous appeal of the medium, on aesthetic surface:

For, as art addresses not pure sense, still less the pure intellect, but the "imaginative reason" through the senses, there are differences of kind in aesthetic beauty, corresponding to differences in kind of the gifts of sense themselves. Each art, therefore, having its own special mode of reaching the imagination, its own special responsibilities to its material. One of the functions of aesthetic criticism is to define these limitations; to estimate the degree in which a given work of art fulfills its responsibilities to its special material; to note in a picture that true pictorial charm, which is neither a mere poetical thought or sentiment, on the one hand, nor a mere result of communicable skill in colour or design, on the other.[23]

This may appear to be rudimentary to us, but we must recall that in Pater's earlier writing on art and most of Ruskin's, pictures were interpreted in terms of their illustrative values. Ruskin was not entirely consistent on this point, but he often assumed the substance of painting and poetry to be identical, and the difference in medium a minor difference in "language." Pater is now very explicit in ruling out a literary approach:

It is in the criticism of painting that this truth most needs enforcing for it is in popular judgments of pictures that false generalization of all art into forms of poetry is most prevalent. To suppose that all is mere technical acquirement in delineation or touch, working through and addressing itself to the intelligence, on the one side, or a merely poetical, or what may be called literary interest, addressed also to the pure intelligence, on the other;—this is the way of most spectators, and of many critics, who have never caught sight, all the time, of that true pictorial quality which lies between (unique pledge of the possession of the gift) the inventive or creative handling of pure line and colour, which, as almost always in Dutch painting, as often also in the works of Titian and Veronese, is quite independent of anything definitely poetical in the subject it accompanies. It is the *drawing*—the design projected from that peculiar pictorial temperament or consititution, in which while it may possibly be ignorant of true anatomical proportions, all things whatever, all poetry, every idea however abstract or obscure, floats up as a visible scene or image; it is the colouring—that weaving of just perceptible gold threads of light through the dress, the flesh, the atmosphere in Titian's *Lace-girl* —the staining of the whole fabric of the thing with a new delightful physical quality. This drawing, then—the arabesque traced in the air by Tintoret's flying figures, by Titian's forest branches; this colouring—the magic conditions of light and hue in the atmosphere of Titian's *Lace-girl* or Rubens' *Descent from the Cross:*—these essential pictorial qualities must first of all delight the sense, delight it as directly and sincerely as a fragment of Venetian glass; and through this delight only like the medium of whatever poetry or science may be beyond them, in the intention of the composer. In its primary aspect, a great picture has no more definite message for us than an accidental play of sunlight and shadow for a moment, on the wall or floor.[24]

In designating the essential pictorial quality to lie midway between technique of execution and literary interest, Pater has defined the area which was to absorb the attention of the formalist critics of the present century—the area of "significant form," perhaps the most problematic question in modern art criticism. Pater specifies both the creative and the essential aspects of pictorial form, but he does not actually succeed in linking form and expression. A lacuna exists between the formalist approach implicit in the Giorgione essay and the idea of style he formulated later in connection with literary art.

It will be noted that Pater makes a reservation concerning formalism, that it constitutes a primary, in the sense of preliminary, stage of criticism, that from this primary and essential "condition" we may proceed to the literary or scientific interest of the picture. This caution is due to a certain conservatism on Pater's part which can be explained by the nature of the art with which he is dealing—representational art containing a relatively high degree of naturalism. It is all the more remarkable, then, that he proceeds to what is actually propaganda for an art of pure form, in which the pictorial qualities are primary in the sense of principal. Pater's rationale is based on the analogy of music, an idea which was widespread in nineteenth-century Symbolist aesthetics, and recurs in certain twentieth-century theories of nonfigurative art. Pater's remains the classic statement of the case:

All art constantly aspires towards the condition of music. For while in all other works of art it is possible to distinguish the matter from the form, and the understanding can always make this distinction, yet it is the constant effort of art to obliterate it. That the mere matter of a poem, for instance—its subject, its given incidents or situations; that the mere matter of a picture—

the actual circumstances of an event, the actual topography of a landscape—should be nothing without the form, the spirit, of the handling, that this form, this mode of handling should become an end in itself, should penetrate every part of the matter:—this is what all art constantly strives after, and achieves in different degrees.[25]

The idea of "form as an end in itself" is much more important both historically and critically than that of art for art's sake, with which Pater is usually associated. For though one may regard the doctrine of pure poetry as a minor or negligible literary phenomenon, one cannot take a comparable attitude toward the parallel movement in the visual arts. It is possible to take issue with the statement that all art constantly aspires toward the condition of music. For stylistic reasons, perhaps, Pater employs the declarative rather than the optative form, thereby making it more absolute than he intended. He is voicing an hypothesis which, though not eccentric, does not adequately account for the historical development of the visual arts. Furthermore, analogy with music is ambiguous, in that the status of musical form and content remains a baffling problem in aesthetics. If one regards music as an art of pure form devoid of content, Pater's statement looks forward to the nonobjective art of our time. But it is more likely, in the light of the application of his theory to the school of Giorgione, that Pater thinks of music as embodying fusion of form and content so complete that neither can be extricated from the other. While the notion of an organic fusion of form and content is one of the most fruitful discoveries of modern critical theory and one that is almost universally accepted, it is a difficult hypothesis to demonstrate. An obvious example is the interaction of meter and meaning in a poem. We may be intuitively convinced of a unified effect, but, as I. A. Richards has observed, the metrical and the semantic analysis must proceed on planes which never actually converge. The interaction of matter and form in representational art may be more intimate than in poetry, but it still presents great difficulties for critical analysis. One rather dramatic solution of the problem is to declare the irrelevance of subject matter. In practice, the nonformal elements keep intruding themselves, as Roger Fry discovered. At any rate a purely formalistic approach would appear to operate best on purely formal art.

Pater's version of formalism is handled with considerable discretion and tact. Far from arguing the irrelevance of subject matter, he demonstrated that in the case of Giorgione, the formal aim, which is the principal or even exclusive aim, is achieved by the control of subject matter. Giorgione's distinction is his discovery of *genre,* a special kind of subject matter wholly amenable to the formal ends of the artist, since it makes no historical, theological, literary, or naturalistic claims on his fantasy. It is significant, in the light of twentieth-century aesthetics, that Pater traces the formalist motive of Giorgione to its origin in Byzantine art:

The beginnings of Venetian painting link themselves to the last, stiff, half-barbaric splendors of Byzantine decoration, and are but the introduction into the crust of marble and gold on the walls of *Duomo* of Murano, or of Saint Marks, of a little more human expression. And throughout the course of its later development, always subordinate to architectural effect, the work of the Venetian school never escaped from the influence of its beginnings. Unassisted, and therefore unperplexed, by naturalism, religious mysticism, philosophical theories, it had no Giotto, no Angelico, no Botticelli. Exempt from the stress of thought and sentiment, which taxes so severely the resources of the generations of Florentine artists, those earlier Venetian painters down to Carpaccio and Bellini, seem never for a moment to have been tempted even to lose sight of their art in its strictness, or to forget that painting must be before all things decorative, a thing for the eye, a space of colour on the wall, only more dexterously blunt than the markings of its precious stone or the chance interchange of sun and shade upon it—this to begin and end with—whatever

higher matter of thought, or poetry, or religious reverie, might
play its part therein, between.[26]

Pater's criticism of the visual arts encompasses both of the
dominant aesthetic approaches of our own time—the expressionist and the formalist—but does not really succeed in
achieving a synthesis. His idea of expressiveness is primarily
the product of his literary experience, his idea of form that
of his visual sensibility. He does not find Giorgione's work
to be less expressive than that of the Florentines: the difference lies in the degree to which formal and expressive elements are fused. For him, Giorgione's pictures constitute
"painted poems," in which the literary element is so refined,
so idealized (so remote from actuality) that it is no longer
felt to be an intrusion upon the purely visual, or "decorative,"
element. Pater appears to be on the verge of "significant
form," but it is doubtful that without the example of Post-
Impressionist art he could have arrived at the absolute formalism of Clive Bell and Roger Fry, or without a knowledge
of nonobjective art at the synthesis or formalism and expressionism which is the singular achievement of Sir Herbert
Read.

# C L I V E   B E L L

1881    Born September 16, into a county family. His parents valued money, respectability, conventional success, hunting, shooting, and fishing, none of which counted for much in Bell's scale of values. Bell was educated at a preparatory school and at Marlborough.

1898    Entered Trinity College, Cambridge, on a scholarship.

1899    With Saxon Sydney-Turner, Leonard Woolf, Lytton Strachey, Thoby Stephen, and A. J. Robertson, founded the Midnight Society, an undergraduate reading club. This group was the nucleus of the intellectual movement later to be known as Bloomsbury. At Cambridge, G. E. Moore, the philosopher, was a dominant influence in Bell's life and ideas.

1902    Obtained B.A. degree with second-class honors. Granted the Earl of Derby studentship by Trinity College. Spent the period October, 1902, to August, 1903, in the Record Office, London, preparing a dissertation on British policy at the Congress of Verona.

1903    Spent summer in British Columbia on a hunting expedition with his father.

1904    Went to Paris in January to continue his historical researches at the Archives Nationales. Became passionately interested in pictures, especially those of the Impressionist painters. Met the English painter Gerald Kelly, from whom he learned about the technique of oil painting and lithography. Friendship with J. W. Morrice, the Canadian painter, who introduced him to the work of Matisse. His most intimate friend in Paris was the painter Roderick O'Connor, who exhibited at the Salon d'Automne and Les Indépendants, who had known Gauguin, and whose remarkable taste and judgment opened up for Bell the work of the advanced painters of this era.

1905   Lived in St. Symphorien, a village near Tours.

1906   Read for the bar in Chambers in the Temple. Met Maynard Keynes. Became engaged to Vanessa Stephen, the painter, eldest daughter of Sir Leslie Stephen, sister of Virginia Woolf.

1907   Married Vanessa Stephen. Met Walter Sickert, whom he considers to be the greatest English painter since Constable.

1910   Met Roger Fry. Joined Roger Fry and Desmond McCarthy in Paris to select pictures for the first Post-Impressionist exhibition in London.

1911   Was taken to Picasso's studio in Montparnasse by Gertrude Stein. Has remained a close friend of Picasso's.

1914   Published *Art*. This work, which presented Bell's aesthetic theory, had originally been planned as part of a larger project, *The New Renaissance,* the completion of which was frustrated by the outbreak of war.

1915   Published *Peace at Once,* a pacifist pamphlet.

1916–   Shared a house at 46 Gordon Square with Maynard
1918    Keynes. Friendship with Duncan Grant, David Garnett, Francis Birrell, Raymond Mortimer, Aldous Huxley, T. S. Eliot, Ralph Partridge.

1919 Paris. Friendship with Derain, Braque, André Salmon, Dunoyer de Segonzac, Despiau, Jean Marchand, Kisling, Marcoussis, Stravinsky, Ansermet. Met Satie and Poulenc through Jean Cocteau. Met André Gide, Duhamel, Jules Romains, Louis Jouvet through Copeau and Vildrac. Acquaintance with Léger, Lipchitz, Pascin, and Metzinger. In the summer of 1919, saw Picasso, Derain, Stravinsky, and Ansermet in London, during the visit of the Diaghilev ballet.

1922 Published *Since Cézanne,* a collection of essays on modern French painting. Published an article on Virginia Woolf's *Jacob's Room* in *Vanity Fair* (New York).

1923 *On British Freedom.*

1927 *Landmarks in Nineteenth Century French Painting.*

1928 *Civilization,* an essay.

1929 *Proust,* one of the earliest studies in English.

1931 *An Account of French Painting.*

1934 *Enjoying Pictures,* an introspective account of the author's experiences in the National Gallery.

1936 Made a Chevalier of the Legion of Honor.

1956 *Old Friends:* essays on Walter Sickert, Lytton Strachey, Maynard Keynes, Virginia Woolf, T. S. Eliot.

IT is generally assumed that the modern movement in painting is revolutionary to an extent unprecedented in the history of painting and unparalleled in the other arts. According to one school of thought, the character of modern art is defined not by radical innovations in style and technique, which have been multiform, nor by the drastic and massive rejection of the imitative function of art, but by a new consciousness of its ontological status, its mode of existence. For André Malraux, the chief exponent of this view, modern painting is for the first time, "simply painting." Modern art has both realized and proclaimed that state of absolute autonomy which, in the art of the past, had been a surreptitious or unconscious aim, and has thus liberated painting from dependence on any meaning or reference extraneous to itself.

The impact of modern art on criticism and aesthetics has not been uniform. Malraux represents an extreme position, but twentieth-century writing on art generally reflects both a realignment of taste and a revolution from the art of the past which amounts almost to a retroactive version of history.

Modern art, specifically the French Post-Impressionists, provided Clive Bell with the ultimate revelation concerning the formal basis of art, toward which Pater and the other nineteenth-century aesthetes had been tending. No less than Pater, Bell addressed an audience whose culture was principally literary. Part of his problem was to disentangle painting from its literary encumbrances, a task which had been only partially and imperfectly accomplished by Pater. Isolated on the whole from contemporary art, Pater perceived in traditional painting precisely that which the revolutionary art of the following century has made into its leading principle— that subject matter is invariably subordinate to the artists' other interests. Pater never actually confronted the crucial questions involving the aesthetic status of representation in the visual arts and the relationship of representation and form, but he is extremely perceptive concerning Giorgione's musicalization of painting, arrived at by a subtle matching of decorative and expressive means. Giorgione achieves equilibrium by choice of a subject which is, so to speak, recessive;

it is subservient to the aesthetic appeal of the work. By inference, an excessively assertive subject matter would be in opposition to its formal constitution. Pater, however, stops short of Bell's unqualified assertion that not only literary subject matter, but indeed representation itself, is irrelevant to aesthetic experience.

We can discern in Pater's art criticism a progression, by no means clear-cut, from the search for specific aesthetic virtue in the painter's temperament to an identification of aesthetic quality with pictorial (that is, formal) elements, but he remained faithful to his original conviction that aesthetic speculation in the abstract was fruitless. There is no trace of relativism or suspense of judgment in Bell's aesthetic system, first enunciated in a book entitled *Art* (1914). It presents a single, universal hypothesis by means of which the aesthetic existence of all works of visual art may be tested. Bell dared to isolate and define what had so far eluded or baffled nearly all investigators, the "essence" of visual art. The element common to all works of art is "significant form"; unlike beauty, a concept which is wholly abandoned in Bell's aesthetics, it is found only in works of art, never in nature. The idea was stunning in its boldness and simplicity, and for at least two decades it was the leading doctrine in art criticism. It served as a talisman for explaining the powerful yet disturbing effects of the new art, often achieved by ignoring or violating existing notions of beauty. The brilliance of an hypothesis, however, is no guarantee of its utility. Significant form figures in Bell's subsequent writings on art as the central tenet, an article of faith, but on the whole he never actually shaped it into a critical instrument for the elucidation of individual works. It remained for Roger Fry to test the hypothesis in the framework of objective formal analysis.

Formalism as such is a relatively late idea in art criticism, appearing not earlier than the nineteenth century; however, the idea of form as design or structure distinguishable from the subject matter of representational painting is at least as old as the Renaissance. Form in the latter sense can be grasped by the intellect and comprehended according to certain categories of order, such as unity, harmony, balance. But significant form is something that cannot be rationally apprehended or even intuited; it can only be felt, and the warrant of its presence in a work of art is the magnitude of emotion it evokes in the beholder. Modern formalism is usually associated with the classical temper and with reaction against the expressionist phase of romanticism, but Bell's aesthetics has a certain affinity with romantic aesthetics. By designating form itself as the bearer of significance, Bell counteracts the stigma that it attached to the idea of form as decoration, that is, as a purely visual pattern devoid of emotional force. But whereas Ruskin conceived of art as expressive of the totality of man's spiritual life, Bell restricts aesthetic phenomenon to an emotion so specialized, so peculiar to itself that the term *expression* is hardly applicable. The emotive basis of significant form together with its autonomous status leads to a variant of aestheticism which surpasses in intensity Pater's refined hedonism. Aesthetic emotion is something far beyond the satisfactions of a cultivated sensibility; at its best, it is no less than ecstasy, comparable in intensity, if not in quality, to the ecstasies of physical love and religion. Bell is quite explicit in equating aesthetic and religious experience:

That it is a means to a state of exaltation is unanimously agreed, and that it comes from the spiritual depth of man's nature is hardly contested. The appreciation of art is certainly a means to ecstasy . . . Art is, in fact, a necessity to and a product of the spiritual life. . . . Religion, like art, is concerned with the world of emotional reality, and with material things only, in so far as they are emotionally significant. For the mystic, as for the artist, the physical universe is a means to ecstasy. . . . Religion, as I understand it, is an expression of the individual's sense of the emotional significance of the universe; I should not be surprised to find that art was the expression of the same thing . . . Art and religion belong to the same world.[1]

Unlike those who advocated an aesthetic attitude to life as a means of surmounting the nothingness of existence, Bell does not believe that aesthetic awareness can be acquired or cultivated. The capacity for experiencing aesthetic emotion is presumably inborn; furthermore, it is exceedingly rare. The artist capable of producing significant form possesses it, but in our culture the vast majority of those who look at pictures react only to the illustrative values of painting and to their sentimental associations. Perhaps least susceptible to significant form are the members of the educated classes, in whom an excessively literary and intellectual culture has brought about a kind of visual atrophy. The average civilized person, according to Bell, is so habituated to seeing labels rather than things that he is virtually insensible to form. An important distinction is to be made between perception as a conceptual activity and as an emotional activity. Many children and primitive people retain a capacity for acute emotional response to visual forms, but except for artists and those gifted with exceptional sensibility civilized adults no longer possess it.

The primitivist strain in Bell's philosophy of art is a familiar one in modern art theory. It appears in Ruskin's notion of the "innocent eye," of vision uncorrupted by conceptual knowledge. In our own time, Sir Herbert Read has been its most vocal exponent. But whereas Read's concern over the atrophy of sensibility in civilized societies has moved him to advocate a drastic reform of education, Bell is content to regard art as the province of the elect, the fortunate few. He remains aloof from the movement initiated by Ruskin and continued by William Morris and Herbert Read to establish an art philosophy upon the broadest possible so-

cial base. The countermovement, which may be very roughly
designated as aristocratic, is visible in Pater's tendency to isolate art from the common concerns of mankind and to make
it the property of those who possess the leisure and the means
to cultivate a life of exquisite sensations. Not only does Bell
restrict authentic experience of the visual arts to those capable
of a direct emotional response to significant form, but he
adopts an extreme position respecting the separation of art
and life. The aesthetic emotion which underlies both the artist's creation of significant form and the spectator's quasi-
mystical rapture is distinct in kind from all other human
emotions and unrelated to them.

The theory of significant form reveals a certain kinship
with romantic aesthetics in its primitivist implication and in
its specification of the emotional basis of art, but it repudiates
romantic expressionism—the idea that art communicates personal or subjective emotions, in the ordinary sense. Bell's
doctrine is "classical" to the extent that it calls for an impersonal art. It bears a certain resemblance to the ideas of
T. S. Eliot's essay "Tradition and the Individual Talent," in
which a distinction is made between the personal emotions
of the poet and his feelings for the objects which compose
the true material of poetry. Actually Bell goes beyond the
idea of an impersonal art to that of a dehumanized art, which
can never be realized in poetry:

In great poetry it is the formal music that makes the miracle.
The poet expresses in verbal form an emotion but distantly related
to the words set down. But it is related; it is not purely artistic
emotion. In poetry form and significance are not everything; the
form and the content are not one . . . The form is burdened with
an intellectual content, and that content is a mood that mingles
with and reposes on the emotions of life. That is why poetry,
though it has its raptures, does not transport us to that remote
aesthetic beatitude in which, freed from humanity, we are up-
stayed by musical and pure visual form.[2]

The state of aesthetic beatitude induced by significant form can be established by empirical evidence, but does not lend itself readily to rational analysis or explication. The difficulty is compounded by Bell's insistence on the absolute uniqueness of aesthetic experience. It can be comprehended only by analogy: In order to appreciate a work of art, Bell informs us, no prior knowledge of life is required, no knowledge of ideas, no repertory of emotion. The act of aesthetic contemplation is utterly distinct from ordinary experience. For its duration other human interests are suspended, memory is arrested, and the stream of life is transcended. Nothing else is comparable to it, unless it be the state of mind of the pure mathematician absorbed in his studies.

The practical effect of an aesthetics postulated on the absolute autonomy of aesthetic experience is to invalidate the traditional concerns of criticism. The emotion which constitutes that experience eludes the grasp of the psychologist. One of the earliest critics of Bell's position was I. A. Richards, who declared in the *Principles of Literary Criticism* that psychology does not recognize a set of specialized emotions stemming exclusively from the work of art, and that the emotions experienced in a picture gallery are not different in kind from those we experience outside the gallery. The difference lies in the organization to which ordinary emotions are normally submitted in the work of art. In refutation of Richards, Bell can only fall back on the empirical argument, imputing that Richards has never experienced the authentic aesthetic "thrill," and disclaiming responsibility for its explanation:

The thrill is the beginning and the essential cause of all aesthetic experience be it ecstasy or happiness. . . . The thrill . . . seems to come most easily to one already in a mood which only the thrill can provoke. . . . What induces the mood in which the first shock is received? As I am an aesthete and not a psychologist it is no part of my duty to answer.[3]

Bell is less concerned with the psychology of the creative process than with that of aesthetic response. For him, aesthetics is properly concerned only with the work of art considered as an object and with emotion induced by the object. It is superfluous, therefore, to inquire into the state of mind of the maker of the object. Furthermore, since the phenomenon of significant form is both absolute and universal, and hence not subject to external conditioning whether psychological or environmental, Bell would exclude from art criticism the apparatus of art history, both technical and sociological. This exclusion is more easily proclaimed in theory than carried out in practice. In his own survey of nineteenth-century French painting Bell violates his own precept, partly, as I shall show, because he lacks the technical knowledge requisite for thorough formal analysis. But Bell's shortcomings as a critic do not invalidate the propriety of the intrinsic approach, according to which archaeological, historical, and biographical data are strictly ancillary to the central act of criticism.

The risk incurred by the idea of aesthetic autonomy carried to its extreme point is that of abrogating criticism, of removing the work of art entirely from the province of rational discourse. Bell was willing to face this risk: "A picture by Bonnard escapes from its subject, and from its author too. . . . It is just this independent life of its own that gives to a work of art its peculiar character and power. Unluckily, about this detached life, about a work considered as a work of art, there is little or nothing to be said. . . ." [4] But despite his somewhat arcane notion of aesthetic emotion, Bell does manage to say a great deal about art, about individual works, and about art considered historically. He even admits, in the most general way, a causal connection between art and society. Not that the social or cultural milieu can have a discernible effect on the form of the individual work, but the great ages of religion are also the great ages of art, since both religion and art are animated by the release of feeling, by spiritual ferment. He voices the commonly held conviction that the history of art is an accurate index of spiritual history. While allowing that art is caused by spiritual states, Bell is very explicit and emphatic in denying that it is the expression of a spiritual state. It is to be regarded rather as a "manifestation" of spiritual activity. He resolves the ambivalence of form and expression which characterized the romantic aesthetics of Ruskin and Pater by confining the reference of form to emotions which are exclusively associated with form. Bell accepts the hypothesis of Tolstoy's *What is Art?* that the function of art is the communication of emotion from the consciousness of the artist to that of the beholder, but if we ask what emotion is conveyed by significant form, we learn that it communicates itself. The argument is almost impossibly tautological. As previously noted, the designation of form as significant served to avert the imputation that formalism involves only the surface qualities of a work of visual art—the decorative elements which provide sensuous pleasure —but failed to penetrate beneath that surface to its spiritual core. The notable insight of Bell was that the so-called decorative elements are themselves spiritual phenomena. We are justified, then, in taking "significant" to mean spiritually significant; yet a certain ambiguity inheres in Bell's use of the term "significant." Evidently form is to be taken as important, momentous. But since in its primary sense the term denotes "meaningful," "expressive," one is normally inclined to associate importance with import.

Bell's exposition of the idea of significant form is straightforward and simple:

The starting point for all systems of aesthetics must be the personal experience of a peculiar emotion. The objects that provoke this emotion we call works of art . . . If we can discover some quality common and peculiar to all the objects that provoke it, we shall have solved what I take to be the central problem of aesthetics . . . Only one answer seems possible—significant form. In each [work of art] lines and colours combined in a particular way, certain forms and relations of forms, stir our aesthetic emotions. These relations and combinations of lines and colours, these aesthetically moving forms, I call "Significant Form." [5]

The simplicity of the formulation, however, is achieved at the expense of logical rigor. The only reliable evidence for the presence of significant form in a work is subjective emotion, which is identified as being completely distinct from all other kinds of emotion. Yet significant form is not merely a synonym for aesthetic emotion. It is immanent in the work and exists independently of the beholder, being the product of aesthetic emotion experienced by the artist.

Bell's identification of significant form with a specific kind of emotion is not to be confused with the familiar theory of art as an expression of emotion. He does concede that a work of art containing significant form may have its inception in the artist's desire to express emotion. An artist looking at certain objects (the contents of a room, let us say) may perceive them as pure forms existing in a certain relationship to each other and may feel for them an emotion which he desires to express. But the expression of emotion is not the signal or definitive feature of a work of visual art. That lies only in the power of the work to evoke aesthetic emotion in the beholder.

It might be inferred from Bell's statement concerning the artist's perception of pure form that form in the visual arts is abstracted from either natural or man-made objects. This might serve to provide an objective reference for grasping the nature of form. But Bell is very clear on this point. Whereas the forms and formal relations of a painting may be derived from objects presented to the artist's vision, he is not bound by that vision. The source of his forms is internal. Hence the emotional (that is, aesthetic) effectiveness of nonobjective works like a Sung vase, or a Romanesque church.

Significant form has no meaning apart from the work of art. It does not exist in nature. While natural forms may be beautiful and thus produce emotions in us, these emotions are not the same as those aroused by a work of art. Lest his assertion be regarded as excessively categorical, Bell offers a tentative explanation of the difference: significant form conveys emotion felt by the artist, while beauty as the property of objects conveys nothing.

Bell's aesthetics appears to lie midway between an excessively purist formalism and an incipient expressionism which threatens the notion of pure form. Realizing the unsatisfactory nature of a hypothesis which explains form in terms of emotions which in turn refer only to form, he makes a single, tentative venture out of the closed circle into which his speculations have led. The significance of anything as an end in itself suggests to him that significant form is that kind of form behind which we glimpse a sense of ultimate reality. The idea of the cognitive value of form opens vast possibilities, all of which lead away from the conception of art as autotelic and threaten the basic premise of Bell's aesthetics. Lacking the philosophical equipment for coping with the suggestion, he refrains from elaborating it. In his last book on painting, *Enjoying Pictures,* in which he gives a full account of the occurrence of aesthetic emotion based on introspection, the frame of reference is hedonistic rather than metaphysical or mystical.

Bell's aesthetics is more impressive for its boldness than for its logic or utility. In retrospect, forty years after he had formulated it, significant form appeared to him to have been an "impetuous" doctrine. But its importance in the history of taste should not be underestimated. In the early decades of this century it prepared the way for the wide acceptance of modern art and the almost total revision of attitudes toward art which that acceptance entailed. The central issue was, of course, the matter of representation. The great achievement of nineteenth-century romantic art criticism had been its discovery of the fact—known by genuine artists in all periods but ignored by the contemporary public and by the pseudo-artists who catered to the preferences of that public—that the merit of a painting did not consist in its representational accuracy or resemblance but in its imaginative force and emotional effect. Post-romantic authorities went further in subordinating representation to form conceived of in terms of the sensuous medium of painting. As we have seen in connection with both Ruskin and Pater, representation occupies an ambiguous status. In one case it is subordinated to expression, in the other, to form; but in neither is it regarded as dispensable. Pater adumbrated the organicity of the form-content relationship, in which the subject matter of painting is so completely absorbed in its form that it no longer asserts itself as an element of interest. Bell goes farther than any previous theorist in denying aesthetic value to representation of the visible or to the associations evoked by the objects represented. Logically, his theory calls for abstract art, in which the element of representation is reduced to a minimum, or nonobjective painting, in which it is entirely dispensed with. But whereas an important segment of contemporary painters have acted upon these premises, Bell himself is not a partisan of non-objective or abstract art. Representation is not inimical to significant form; it is simply irrelevant to it. The enlightened spectator, the aesthete, reacts only to the form in a representational painting. He experiences it as an abstraction.

In theory, Bell is committed to the proposition that representation as such neither detracts from significant form, nor conflicts with it in any way. Representation then, should not be regarded as intrinsically bad or harmful. In the over-all design of a painting, a realistic form may be just as significant as an abstract form, but the aesthetic value of the realistic form pertains only to the form, not to the representation. As far as significant form is concerned, representation is simply irrelevant. It should not be forgotten, however, that the idea of significant form was probably revealed to Bell by the Post-Impressionist works which had been exhibited in England only a few years before the publication of his first book on art, and that public taste had not advanced very far from "that darkest hour when men confounded imitation with art"—the era of the late nineteenth-century academy picture, freighted with narrative content and executed with photographic realism. Representation constitutes a danger to the purity of aesthetic emotion in both artist and spectator:

That there is an irrelevant or descriptive element in many great works of art is not in the least surprising. Representation is not of necessity baneful, and highly realistic forms may be extremely significant. Very often, however, representation is a sign of weakness in an artist. A painter too feeble to create forms that provoke more than a little aesthetic emotion will try to eke out that little by suggesting emotions of life. To evoke the emotions of life he must use representation . . . in the spectator a tendency to seek, behind form, the emotions of life is a sign of a defective sensibility always.[6]

Bell's proscription of the "literary" or sentimental content of representational art as irrelevant to the emotion provoked by pictorial form is quite plausible. But the total irrelevance of representation is more difficult to maintain, and Bell does admit one aspect of representation as vital to painting.

As an awareness of space as three-dimensional is essential to the appreciation of most architectural forms, to perceive a solid form such as a cube or rhomboid as a flat pattern is to diminish its significance as form. Paintings which would be "insignificant" if seen as flat patterns actually evoke profound emotion when viewed as related planes. The representation of three-dimensional space is therefore to be regarded as an exception to the general rule of the irrelevance of representation. This concession is a serious breach in the assumed autonomy of aesthetic experience and its corollary—the conception of significant form as unrelated to anything other than itself. By admitting the psychology of space perception as relevant to aesthetics, Bell may be excluding the "emotions of life," but he does not exclude the human consciousness. Herein lies the possibility of an approach to aesthetics which would enable the critic to perceive art in relation to general human experience and thus escape the vicious circle imposed by an absolute formalism. To concede the psychological determination of art would mean the abandonment of the hypothesis concerning the autonomy of aesthetic experience. By observing that space representation, while not irrelevant, is also not essential to significant form, Bell avoids its full implication for aesthetics.

Despite its claim to universality, Bell's aesthetics was not conceived in a vacuum. His afterthought concerning space representation reveals a marked preference for a certain kind of form, specifically that embodied in the work of Cézanne. It would not be too far-fetched to describe Bell's aesthetics as an attempt to provide a rationale for Cézanne's epoch-making formal discoveries. For Cézanne's real achievement was his recognition of the relative autonomy of pictorial forms with respect to the unselective evidence provided by the lax and nonaesthetic perception of natural forms; the creation of pictorial forms involves, in addition to perception, the "realisation" of the artist's sensations. It is not improbable that the origin of significant form can be found in Cézanne's conscientious but not always perfectly lucid attempt to articulate his art; Bell's notion of aesthetic emotion would appear to be nearly equivalent to Cézanne's "sensations." Inasmuch as Cézanne's painting and, to a lesser extent, his theories, determined the development of that whole phase of modern art known as Post-Impressionism, Bell's aesthetic theories are by no means eccentric; they illuminate the practice of those artists who, departing from Cézanne, were almost exclusively concerned with formal problems. They are less applicable to the work of the Post-Impressionists after 1914, to the surrealist elements in Picasso, for instance, and in general to those important phases of modern art which did not stem from France.

Although the formalist aesthetics, as previously noted, precludes an historical approach to art in the generally accepted sense, Bell provides in *Art* an historical survey which is keyed to the doctrine of significant form. It is chiefly interesting today as an accurate index of the revolution in taste which was effected by the emergence of the modern movement. The application of Cézanne's insights into the nature of form by the Post-Impressionists happened to coincide with the new enthusiasm for primitive art which had been rediscovered by the Post-Impressionist painters themselves. Recognition of the aesthetic value of African sculpture appeared to be a striking vindication of significant form, since the twentieth-century European who was moved by these works had no knowledge of their function, their religious or magical significance. Perhaps the most obvious feature of these objects was their almost total discontinuity with the canon of beauty which had dominated European taste for at least five centuries.

In Bell's history of art, significant form and Renaissance illusionism are viewed as antagonists:

Primitives produce art because they must; they have no other motive but a passionate desire to express their sense of form. Untempted, or incompetent to create illusions, to the creation of form they devote themselves entirely. Presently, however, the artist is joined by a patron and a public, and soon there grows up a demand for a "speaking likeness." While the gross herd still clamors for likeness, the choicer spirits begin to affect an admiration for cleverness and skill. The end is in sight. In Europe we watch art sinking, by slow degrees, from the thrilling design of Ravenna to the tedious portraiture of Holland, while the grand proportion of Romanesque and Norman architecture becomes Gothic juggling in stone and glass. Before the late noon of the Renaissance art was almost extinct.[7]

Bell's graph of the decline and fall of European art may be seen as a continuation and revision of tendencies initiated by Ruskin more than a half-century before. Making a distinction between truth, by which he sometimes meant emotion, and imitative skill, Ruskin had undermined the hitherto undisputed supremacy of High Renaissance art. But where Ruskin viewed thirteenth-century Gothic as the apex of European art and everything subsequent to it as decadence, Bell locates the summit in the sixth-century mosaics of Ravenna, "the primitive and supreme summit of the Christian slope." Except for a lapse marked by the iconoclastic movement in the eighth-century Church, Byzantine art remained until the twelfth century the greatest achievement of European art, surpassing the art of the greatest periods of Egypt, Crete, and Greece, and producing more great works between the years 500 and 900 than Europe produced between 1450 and 1850.

Contrary to the preponderant opinion of his contemporaries, Bell regards Gothic art not as a great achievement, but as the beginning of the decline of art. For him, the Gothic cathedral is a *tour de force,* calculated to impress one with the skill of the builder, but totally deficient in pure form. Furthermore, the emotions it evokes—the sense of mystery and power—belong to the realm of melodrama rather than aesthetics. In painting, the decadence is manifest in Giotto, who is unfavorably contrasted with Cimabue, who was closer to the Byzantine tradition and hence to significant form. According to Bell, it was Giotto's humanism, his preoccupation with the humanity of his figures, that ruined his

art. It should be noted that representation itself is not the
issue here. What Bell objects to is the diversion of the painter's interest to the depiction of what Roger Fry called psychological or dramatic states, that is, to "literary" description.
Although Bell views the Renaissance as a whole as a disastrous episode in art history, devoted overwhelmingly to
imitation and scientific picture making, he specifically exempts from the general charge such artists as Masaccio, Masolino, Castagno, Piero della Francesca, Fra Angelico, Uccello,
and Mantegna, whose preoccupation with the technical problems of space representation and perspective induced a passionate concern with form. It was not the scientific and
technical advances, ultimately ruinous, which produced significant form in their work, but the emotion and excitement
which accompanied the new technical discoveries.

In the light of his predisposition to primitive art, Bell's
animus against the Italian Renaissance is not surprising. He
finds the humanistic ideal, preëminently intellectual and
materialistic, to be inimical to visual forms:

[The classical view] showed men they could manage very well
without a soul. It made materialism tolerable by showing how
much can be done with matter and intellect . . . When men had
lost sight of the spirit it covered the body with the garment of
glamour . . . With the Renaissance Europe definitely turns her
back on the spiritual view of life. With that renunciation the
power of creating significant form becomes the inexplicable gift
of the occasional genius. Here and there an individual produces
a work of art, so art comes to be regarded as something essentially
sporadic and peculiar. The artist is reckoned a freak . . . genius-
worship is the infallible sign of an uncreative age. In great ages
. . . where there are many artists art tends to become anonymous.[8]

After the Renaissance the decline continues steadily. The
seventeenth century is rich in individual geniuses, but the
general level is very low. And of the great names—El Greco,

Rembrandt, Velásquez, Vermeer, Rubens, Jordaens, Poussin, Claude, Wren, Bernini—the greatest of them all, Rembrandt, is a typical victim of the age. According to Bell, his innate gift for form and design is submerged by the literary content, by rhetoric and romance, which were demanded by his contemporaries.

Bell passes rapidly over the eighteenth and nineteenth centuries. The eighteenth produced brilliant illustrators in Watteau, Canaletto, Crome, Cotman, Guardi, and Hogarth, but only one authentic master of form, Chardin, who remained uncorrupted by the literary virus. Romanticism in painting is dismissed as a mere variant of neo-classicism, marked by a transfer of subject matter to ruins and medieval history, but not distinguishable in the matter of form. By the middle of the nineteenth century painting had reached its nadir in that staple commodity, the academy picture, exhibited by the acre in official salons. Ingres, Corot, and Daumier are exempted from the general condemnation. Bell at this period of his life took a dim view of the Impressionists on the ground of their failure to produce significant form. The historical importance of the Impressionists for Bell depended not on their "grotesque" theories concerning the nature of light, but on their contribution to the idea of the autonomy of art, teaching people to seek significance in the picture itself instead of searching for it in the emotions and interests of the world outside.

By the time he came to write *Landmarks in Nineteenth Century French Painting* (1927), Bell had become a fervent admirer of the Impressionists, but in his earlier work they are completely overshadowed by Cézanne, "the Christopher Columbus of a new continent of form." Having reached this point in the survey, we realize that Bell's scale of values in judging the art of the past is derived from Cézanne, or more properly the interpretation of Cézanne's significance made by the Post-Impressionist painters between 1904 and 1914.

Bell was inclined at first to regard these years as the start of a new era. We recall that *Art* was originally to have formed part of a much larger work to be titled *The New Renaissance,* treating of the resurgence of spiritual activity in the new century. The war of 1914–1918 put an end to this project as well as to Bell's optimism for his century, but he had no reason in later years to revise his original estimate of Cézanne's contribution to the visual arts.

In his first survey of the history of art, Cézanne occupies a position comparable to that of the first creators of the Ravenna mosaics:

Cézanne discovered methods and forms which have revealed a vista of possibilities to the end of which no man can see . . . At Aix-en-Provence came to him a revelation that has set a gulf between the nineteenth century and the twentieth; for gazing at the familiar landscape, Cézanne came to understand it, not as a mode of light . . . but as an end in itself and an object of intense emotion. Every great artist has seen landscape as an end in itself—as pure form, that is to say; Cézanne has made a generation of artists feel that compared with its significance as an end in itself all else about a landscape is negligible. From that time forward Cézanne set himself to create forms that would express the emotion he felt for what he had learned to see. Science became as irrelevant as subject. Everything can be seen as pure form, and behind pure form lurks the mysterious significance that thrills to ecstasy.[9]

An excess of enthusiasm for Cézanne's forms causes Bell to underestimate both Cézanne's indebtedness to the Impressionists and the importance Cézanne himself attached to the representation of natural structures, but his interpretation of Cézanne's significance for twentieth-century art is perfectly valid.

The revolution effected by Cézanne is first of all a liberation from the demands of verisimilitude. Here Bell is quite consistent with his theoretical assertions concerning the irrelevance of representation to significant form. Cézanne's distortions are not intrinsically significant; they are merely "the external and visible evidence of an inner, spiritual state." For Cézanne reality could be attained only through the medium of the visible world; in his case it did not require the invention of pure abstract forms. Nevertheless, that reality was the result of an entirely personal vision which invested the visible world with a sublime architecture in which every particular bears the stamp of the universal. The great achievement of both his life and his work was the revelation of the autotelic nature of art: painting, the pursuit of the vision, exists in complete isolation from man's urgent activities, from his turbulent history. Cézanne's total concern was with pure form and "that which lying behind pure form gives it significance."

The painters of this century have agreed with Bell's designation of Cézanne as a liberator, and on the whole they have sought to bring to fulfillment the tendencies implicit in his work. The final step in achieving an autonomous art, the abandonment of representation, has been the crucial event in twentieth-century art. While Bell had no theoretical objection to an art of pure form, he manifested little interest in it when it appeared. In his second book on art, *Since Cézanne* (1922), there is some evidence of a retreat from his original position. The modern movement, which was to have ushered in a new era comparable in importance to the "Christian slope" which had animated art for twelve centuries, appears to him to have lost its impetus. Bell regards nostalgically the heroic age of painting (1904–1914), when Picasso and Matisse launched the new movement. He admits that his earlier judgments had been tempered by partisanship, provoked by the violence of those who were opposed to Post-Impressionist art. He defends the new appreciation of exotic and primitive art, but concedes that he had underrated the art of the Renaissance and of the eighteenth and nineteenth centuries. His new and unexpected enthusiasm for Raphael presages not only an indifference to the fate of abstract art but a modification of his earlier, more austere, conception of significant form. He detects in the most recent French painting a tendency

> towards something which I had rather call humanism than humanity . . . [which] does imply, I think, a definite break with Cubism . . . It is not drama or anecdote or sentiment or symbolism that this would bring back to the plastic arts, but rather that mysterious yet recognizable quality in which the art of Raffael excels—a calm, disinterested, and professional concern with the significance of life as revealed directly in form . . . About life, in that sense, the painters of the new generation will, I fancy, have something to say. They will come at it, not by drama or anecdote or symbol, but as all genuine artists have always come at whatever possessed their imagination, by plastic expression, or —if you like old-fashioned phrases—by creating significant form. They will seek the vital principle in all sorts of objects and translate it into forms of every kind. That humane beauty after which Dérain strives, is to be found, I said, in Raffael; it is to be found also in the Parthenon.[10]

From Bell's embarrassment concerning the phrase, it would appear that significant form is more tractable in aesthetic theory than in its critical application. It is fairly evident that he is incapable of disengaging form from those objects of which it is the vital principle. Formalist criticism is possible only when it is implemented by technical knowledge which can both distinguish between formal and non-formal elements and perceive the relation between them. Ruskin had contributed much toward criticism as applied aesthetics in his studies of landscape. Both Pater and Bell provided a rationale for the method of pictorial analysis but lacked practical knowledge. It remained for Roger Fry, among English writers, to provide the formalist hypothesis with the means for a rational elucidation of form and hence for a more objective criticism.

Bell's doctrine, founded as it is on the notion of a specialized, emotional response which can be gauged as to intensity but is otherwise inexplicable, tends to become in the hands of the critic simply the seal of his own preference, not for form, but for certain kinds of form. In Bell's case, the aesthetic of Cézanne, or more accurately, that aesthetic as interpreted by the Post-Impressionists, actually becomes a yardstick by means of which Giotto is ranked below Cimabue, to mention only one of many judgments. The criterion of significant form may suffice to establish the authenticity of a work of art, but it is less useful in discriminating among works which fall within that category. The reference to a humane quality common to Raphael and Derain implies that formal purity is no longer the sole measure of merit. The essay on African sculpture in *Since Cézanne* illustrates the limits of a strictly formal approach. Bell rates African sculpture as a whole below the greatest sculpture—Chinese of the best periods, archaic Greek, Byzantine, Mohammedan, and Romanesque—but above Assyrian, Roman, Indian, Gothic, and Late Renaissance sculpture. Negro sculpture is free of matter which distracts attention from its formal properties, but it is lacking in qualities which are found in the greatest art—profundity of vision, organic unity of complex structures, creative imagination, and finally "that passionate affirmation of a personal vision which we Europeans expect to find in the greatest art." The criteria invoked, it will be noted, are traditional; the last two are generally associated with romantic expressionism.

Walter Pater in the essay "Style" indicated the limits of formalist criticism insofar as literary art is concerned. The aesthetic approach performs the primary defining function, but greatness in literature can be judged only by nonaesthetic—that is, moral—criteria. Bell excludes literature from his aesthetic system; he believes that the formal constituents of literary art are not essential. The corollary view that form is essential in the visual arts is not likely to be contested in our time.

For Bell significant form is an essence, and hence inherently difficult to isolate in a state of purity. From the beginning he was somewhat apprehensive in employing it as the sole criterion of art. In the preface to *Art,* he admits that he has not done full justice to the relation of the essential to the unessential elements in art; it would require someone who was an artist as well as a psychologist to determine the limits of the essential and the unessential, "to tell whether it is easy or difficult or impossible for the artist to destroy every rung in the ladder by which he has climbed to the stars." The crux of Bell's theory is that form is itself significant, actually self-significant. He starts from the position that the very hallmark of significant form is its isolation from all experience extraneous to aesthetic emotion. The theory might quite logically be construed as an apology for an art of pure form, that is, an art purged of nonessential elements. But Bell was actually indifferent to such an art when it finally emerged and showed an increasing preference for "impure" art, for Ingres and Raphael among others.

The idea of unique aesthetic emotion is the weakest link in Bell's formalism, but to refute it is not necessarily to destroy the hypothesis of the primacy of form in the visual arts. The idea of form is central to contemporary speculation on art; the most skillful and most complete formulations of aesthetic theory maintain a delicate balance between the notion of formal autonomy and that of the quasi-linguistic function of form to communicate meanings which lie in the range of affective states. Suzanne Langer's philosophy of art, while preserving the formal identity of each of the individual arts, stresses the universality of symbolic form in all modes of expression. Henri Foçillon's *Vie des Formes* grants that works of visual art belong to a world distinct and peculiar to itself, but in no sense isolated from the human world. The creation of form is seen not as the function of a separate aesthetic faculty, but as an inevitable tendency of human consciousness. "La conscience humaine tend toujours à un langage et même à un style. Prendre conscience, c'est prendre forme."

Viewing the development of aesthetics as a dialectical process, we may view Bell's formalism as a necessary antithesis to the prevailing literary approach to painting. In differentiating pictorial from literary elements, Bell's theory comes very near to depriving form of meaning. Bell's reference to the possibility of form as a revelation of ultimate reality has a certain affinity with the views of certain nonobjective artists like Mondrian and Naum Gabo, who claim cognitive value for their work. On the other hand, Bell's emphasis on the emotional character of form should have made him more receptive to expressionist theory and expressionist art. Bell's insensibility to two of the most important phases of modern art—nonobjective art and Expressionism—was probably determined by his culture and temperament rather than by his aesthetic theories. His sensibility, acute as it is, is susceptible primarily to a single tradition of visual form which we may designate roughly as classical or Mediterranean. His aesthetic culture is oriented almost entirely toward France, and modern art for him means the school of Paris. While that assumption was more plausible in the 1920's than it is today, even within the context of French painting Bell's visual bias is evident. He rates the art of Delacroix and Géricault considerably below that of Ingres and David. His ostensible criterion is that of significant form as against literary associations. Since the work of all of these painters is extremely literary, however, one suspects that he is really voicing an innate preference for architectonic form. Bell's temperament inclined him toward what Heinrich Wölfflin distinguished as static as against dynamic forms. Hence his antipathy toward expressionistic art insofar as it is the product of violent emotion and spontaneous techniques. Bell rates the work of Henri Rousseau above that of an Expressionist like Van Gogh or a Symbolist like Gauguin on the basis of plastic achievement. Bell's rejection of expressionist art does not, however, imply a bias toward the intellectual. His views on symbolism make this clear.

He defines a symbol as an intellectual abbreviation, and hence impossible to integrate in a plastic conception. Since symbols are the product of intellect rather than of emotion, they are to be regarded as "dead matter," unassimilable in the work of art conceived of as an organic whole. To be sure, Bell is thinking of symbols in a narrow, iconographic sense; in the context of his aesthetics, the notion of symbolic form is merely a contradiction in terms.

# ROGER FRY

1866 Born in Highgate, London, December 14, second son of Sir Edward Fry and Mariabella Hodgkin Fry. Both parents were members of old Quaker families. The father, who had a strong scientific bent, entered the legal profession, where he achieved eminence as Lord Justice of Appeal. There was virtually no interest in the arts in the Fry household during Fry's childhood.

1877 Attended school at Sunninghill House, Ascot.

1881 Entered Clifton School, where his main interests were scientific. Formed lifelong friendship with John Ellis McTaggart, who later became famous as a philosopher.

1884 Won an exhibition in science at King's College, Cambridge.

1885 Entered Cambridge. Shared rooms with McTaggart. Met Oscar Browning, the Darwins, Edmund Gosse. Was elected to the Appenines, a literary society. Formed lifelong friendship with G. Lowes Dickinson.

1886 Began to sketch and paint in oils. Attended meetings of the Fine Arts Society in Sidney Colvin's rooms. Was enthusiastic about the Pre-Raphaelite painters. Interest in art encouraged by John Henry Middleton, Slade Professor of Art.

1888 Took his B.A. degree with honors in the natural science examinations. Resolved to become a painter in spite of his father's opposition to art as a profession. As a compromise he remained at Cambridge, dissecting in the laboratory and painting the male nude under the direction of Middleton.

1889 Lived at home in London. Studied painting under Francis Bate. Gave lessons in drawing at Toynbee Hall.

1891 First visit to Italy with Pip Hughes. Worked assiduously in the galleries in Rome and Florence. In Venice, he met John Addington Symonds, the art critic, and Horatio Brown, authority on early Venetian painting, both of whom opened up for him new attitudes toward art.

1892 Painted in the Académie Julian in Paris. Shared rooms with Lowes Dickinson. At this time contemporary French painting made little impression on Fry, who was primarily absorbed by the Italian Renaissance.

1893 Took a house in Beaufort Street, Chelsea, with R. C. Trevelyan. Joined the New English Art Club, the center of serious and advanced artistic life in London. Friendship with G. B. Shaw, Henry Tonks, Sir William Rothenstein, Robert Bridges. Wrote notes on current art for various weeklies.

1894 Became an extension lecturer on art. Gave courses on Italian art in Cambridge, Eastbourne, Brighton. His own painting was not financially successful. Visited Antwerp and Lille to study Rubens. Visited Italy to prepare a book on Giovanni Bellini. On his return to London, designed furniture and interior decoration for friends.

1896 Married Helen Coombe, a fellow exhibitor at the New English Art Club. Wedding trip to France, Tunis, Bizerte, Florence, Naples, Sicily, Venice.

1897  Wife advised to live abroad by London doctors because of lung trouble. Residence in Rome shared by Lowes Dickinson.

1898  Wife developed mental illness. Was committed to an institution in England.

1899  Published *Giovanni Bellini,* a scholarly monograph which exhibited a balance of the technical and theoretical approaches. On his wife's recovery, took a house near Dorking.

1901–  Became art critic of the *Athenaeum.* Published two articles
1902  on Giotto in the *Monthly Review.*

1903  Helped establish the *Burlington Magazine,* a publication devoted to the visual arts.

1904  Failed to obtain the Slade Professorship at Cambridge which fell vacant. Traveled to New York, where he was offered the directorship of the Metropolitan Museum of Art.

1905  Accepted directorship of the Metropolitan Museum and had to decline the directorship of the National Gallery, London, which was offered to him. Published an annotated edition of Reynolds' *Discourses,* in which he wished to show that the classical tradition of European painting was still an essential discipline for the student.

1906  Saw the work of Cézanne for the first time at the New Gallery, London.

1907  Trip to Italy with Pierpont Morgan to purchase art for the Metropolitan.

1910  Severed connection with Metropolitan, principally on account of difficulties with Morgan. Built house in Guild-

ford, Surrey, from his own designs. Learned that his wife's
mental illness was hopeless. Failed to obtain the Slade
Professorship at Oxford. Organized the first Post-Impressionist exhibition at the Grafton Galleries, November. It
contained works by Cézanne, Gauguin, Van Gogh, Picasso,
Signac, Derain, Friesz, Matisse. Violent reaction on the
part of the press and the public.

1911   Refused directorship of the Tate Gallery. Holiday in Con-
stantinople with Clive and Vanessa Bell.

1912   Exhibition of his own work at Alpine Club Gallery. Second
Post-Impressionist Exhibition, Grafton Galleries, October.

1913   Established the Omega workshops in Fitzroy Square, the
purpose of which was to subsidize young artists by means
of the manufacture of well-designed articles of daily use.

1914–  Omega workshops survived the war, in spite of great dif-
1918   ficulties.

1919   Omega workshops closed. Vacation in France, where he
met Derain, Picasso, Vildrac. Formed close friendship with
Charles and Marie Mauron in Saint-Rémy. Took a house
in Camden Town, London, with his sister Margery. Published *Vision and Design,* which was based on his most
important articles written during the previous twenty years.

1920   Exhibition of his own paintings, which was not a financial
success. Began a joint translation of the poetry of Mallarmé
with Charles Mauron.

1923   Published *A Sampler of Castile,* impressions of Spain based
on a trip made in that year.

1926   Published *Transformations,* a collection of speculative and
critical essays.

1927  Failed to obtain Slade Professorship at Oxford. Lectured
      to large audiences at Queen's Hall, London, on the ex-
      hibition of Flemish art at Burlington House. These were
      published in book form as *Flemish Art*. Published *Cézanne*,
      a monograph. Written twice in French and again in Eng-
      lish, this work required more labor than any of his other
      writings. Made honorary fellow of King's College, Cam-
      bridge.

1929  Honorary LL.D. degree, Aberdeen University.

1931  Bought a house in St. Rémy.

1932  Trip to Greece to fill gaps in his knowledge of Greek art.
      Published *The Characteristics of French Art,* a series of
      lectures.

1933  Elected Slade Professor of Art at Cambridge. Delivered
      inaugural lecture on "Art History as an Academic Sub-
      ject." Planned a series of lectures which would apply his
      aesthetic principles to the history of art from Egypt to
      the present day. He had reached Greek art by the time
      of his death. The Cambridge lectures were posthumously
      published in 1939 as *Last Lectures,* with an introduction by
      Sir Kenneth Clark.

1934  Published *Reflections on British Painting,* a series of lec-
      tures. Died in London, September 13, as the result of a fall.


ROGER FRY was the first English art critic to achieve
an international reputation; his work did much to
remove the stigma of provincialism borne by England's previous writers on art. Fry's criticism reveals intellectual gifts of a high order; it possesses a professional,
scholarly cast which was not apparent in his predecessors—

Ruskin, Pater, Symons, George Moore—or in his younger contemporary, Clive Bell. All of them were primarily literary men who at certain stages in their careers had been deeply absorbed in the visual arts. Fry's criticism was his life work, even though he himself regarded it as secondary to his work as a painter. Sir Kenneth Clark has written that insofar as one man can mold the taste of his time, Fry did so. One thinks of Ruskin, who played the same role in his own time. The authority of both Ruskin and Fry derives partly from their expository gifts, but mainly, I think, from the knowledge and visual discipline available to practicing artists. Although both men fell short of their own standards of accomplishment in the visual arts, their criticism gained immeasurably.

Ruskin's sensibility to visual phenomena was both practiced and acute, but as we have seen, his attention to works of art was constantly diverted first by his scientific interests, his knowledge of natural structures, and then by his social and political preoccupations insofar as they entered into his writings on art. It was hardly possible for anyone writing on art in England in the early years of this century to have been unaware of Ruskin's influence. One senses in Fry's criticism a deliberate effort to avoid Ruskin's errors and to counteract his influence. In the development of Fry's ideas one perceives an increasing effort to view the work of art as a finite object, possessing a life of its own, which could be apprehended and discussed in exclusively visual terms. Whether or not that effort was wholly successful, Fry possessed a rare, virtually unique gift for transmitting his own visual experiences in words and at the same time conveying a sense of their importance.

The title of his first collection of essays, *Vision and Design,* comes very close to defining the subjects to which his interests were confined. It had, of course, always been known that painting is primarily an art which involves the eye and that the painter must somehow organize visual materials within a finite area. In the Renaissance "design" was, in fact, synonymous with our term, the "visual arts." Nor are the terms "vision" and "design" unambiguous. Even if vision is read as visual perception, we are still confronted by a baffling and paradoxical psychological phenomenon. Nothing is gained either by converting design into form, which is actually the key term in both Fry's aesthetics and his criticism. Fry was not given to minimizing the difficulties of his métier; near the end of his career he admitted that precision and certainty in these matters were as remote as ever. Despite these misgivings, he did not abandon his course—his steady effort to describe art in terms of the relationship of vision and design, the formal transformation of the materials of visual perception.

It should be noted that in Fry's aesthetics vision is inevitably subordinated to design: the all-important element is form. It is quite accurate to classify him as a formalist; and he is generally regarded as the foremost exponent of that position in aesthetics and criticism. In art criticism formalism has a status somewhat different from that in literary criticism, where it is not in good repute. Insofar as it is distinguished from art history, contemporary art criticism is formalistic to the extent that it eschews "literary" interpretations of paintings and concentrates on pictorial phenomena. However, within the bounds of formalist criticism thus broadly defined there is considerable range of interpretation of the nature and the meaning of form. The primacy of form in the visual arts is no longer disputed, except perhaps by very recent advocates of nonformal or informal art; the dispute centers on the question of the autonomy of form, on whether a strictly formalistic approach can adequately cope with the full implications of form.

Fry's aesthetics, at least in final formulation, is very close to Clive Bell's, but the intellectual tone and temper of his writings is far removed from what we generally regard as aestheticism. Walter Pater's aestheticism was an amalgam of two points of view which are not integrally related. One of these is the conception of form as the basis of art; the other was a variant of Epicureanism which advocates the cultivation of aesthetic awareness as the chief end of existence. Fry's aesthetics is in the direct line of inheritance from the former view; upon it he erected an articulate critical method, whereas for Pater it was little more than a brilliant theoretical *aperçu*. But Fry's renunciation of aestheticism as an ethical philosophy is uncompromising. He is on the side of the late nineteenth-century aesthetes in rejecting Ruskin's demand for a moral evaluation of art, but has no sympathy for the corollary view that art transcends morality. Once he has established his thesis concerning the irrelevance of practical or moral standards in aesthetic affairs, his attitude toward art is that of a disinterested scientific investigator rather than that of the rhapsodist of aesthetic bliss.

The only specifically ethical standard which Fry applies to art is honesty or integrity, the principle by which his own criticism and his intellectual life were regulated. Honesty in art implies, first of all, the artist's devotion to his task, which is the creation of form rather than the evocation of sentiment (this injunction begs the question, since it presupposes the acceptance of Fry's aesthetic premise); in the second place, honesty in the artist implies fidelity, not to facts of nature, as Ruskin sometimes mistakenly insisted, but to his own vision. This latter quality is present in Chardin, a painter highly cherished by Roger Fry:

Chardin's specific gift of eye was no doubt extraordinary, but what gave this gift its full scope were gifts of character and accidents of his social audience . . . I am sometimes inclined to think that honesty is the only one of the moral qualities that affect an artist's work . . . The temptation to an artist is, of course, to try to make people believe that he has had more interesting, more original, more remarkable visual experiences than he really has.[1]

Fry's dislike of the Pre-Raphaelite painters is ascribed to their aestheticism—"a whimsical aestheticism, utterly divorced from life and from good sense . . . they could not think out their problems clearly; they fled from contemporary life instead of facing it and interpreting it. . . . Pre-Raphaelitism had no roots in life . . . an artificial hot-house growth."[2] Fry's reproach of the Pre-Raphaelites in such Ruskinian terms may appear to be totally inconsistent with his formalist position. Yet there is an important distinction between the idea of formal autonomy and that of art as escape. As far as his own involvement in the world of art was concerned, quite apart from his aesthetic theory, Fry is much closer to the tradition of Ruskin than to that of the aesthetes. His enterprise in the Omega workshops recalls the activities of William Morris, with the important differences that Fry's primary motive was practical—to provide an income for young artists—rather than that of social regeneration through art. Fry's social instinct was not so highly developed as Ruskin's, and yet he had in him some of the prophet's zeal as far as art was concerned. Although he never regarded himself as an historical scholar, his knowledge of art was extensive and profound. His services as an expert were sought; his reputation in these matters led to his appointment as director of the Metropolitan Museum in New York. These activities reinforced the authority of his criticism, upon which his influence as a molder of taste was based.

While it is impossible to measure the extent of that influence, its final effect was to bring about the acceptance of modern art by the English public. Clive Bell, who played no small part in the movement, gives Roger Fry full credit for priority. Fry organized the first exhibition of Post-Impressionist painting in London in 1910, and actually invented the name. In spite of the almost universal hostility on the part of the press and the general public which greeted the first exhibit, Fry organized a second in 1912. For those who have witnessed the development of modern art during the last half-century, the violence of initial resistance to it is hard to understand.

Fry had the insight to perceive that the import of modern art was twofold: it brought about not only a radical revision in aesthetics but a revolution in taste. The revelation of Post-Impressionist art led to a changed attitude toward the art of the past and to a new understanding of exotic and primitive art. Clive Bell saw the whole history of European art from the twelfth to the middle of the nineteenth century as a steady decline from the summit of Byzantine achievement; he attributed to Cézanne and the Post-Impressionists the inauguration of a new cycle of great painting. Fry's reaction to the shock of Post-Impressionism was more moderate, the development of his tastes more gradual. Although he eventually arrived at an aesthetic position not far removed from Bell's, he was not prepared to discard his early enthusiasms, his confirmed admiration for the masters of the Italian Renaissance, for Rembrandt, and for seventeenth-century French painting. In the perspective of the last fifty years Fry's tastes and view appear to be not revolutionary, but, if anything, excessively conservative. Not that Fry would have balked at being called a conservative, for his espousal of Post-Impressionism is based on the contention that it represents a return to first principles, to a concern for formal structure which had been the chief glory of the Mediterranean tradition subsequently submerged in the degradation of painting marked by the aims of nineteenth-century illusionism and anecdote.

Although Fry's aesthetic views were so closely allied with those of Bell that they might well be regarded as collabora-

tors, Fry's contribution to art criticism is distinct. Bell so
pithily enunciated the formalist position that for several
decades the concept of "significant form" dominated the
discussion of the visual arts. But Bell was candid enough to
admit that, while he could recognize the presence of significant form by certain affective signals it aroused in him,
he was not able to discuss form as an objective phenomenon.
He thus disclaimed a prime responsibility of the critic, to
confront the individual work of art and to explain its effect.
In his own time, Fry had no rival as an expositor of the
specific properties of works of art.

The empirical cast of Fry's mind is revealed in his deliberate subordination of aesthetics to criticism:

In my work as a critic of art I have never been a pure Impressionist, a mere recording instrument of certain sensations. I have
always had some kind of aesthetic. A certain scientific curiosity
and a desire for comprehension have impelled me at every stage
to make generalisations, to attempt some kind of logical coordination of my impressions. But, on the other hand, I have
never worked out for myself a complete system such as the meta-
physicians deduce from *a priori* principles. I have never believed
that I knew what was the ultimate nature of art. My aesthetic
has been a purely practical one, a tentative expedient, an attempt
to reduce to some kind of order my aesthetic impressions up to
date . . . I have certainly tried to make my judgment as objective
as possible, but the critic must work with the only instrument he
possesses—namely his own sensibility with all its personal equa-
tions.[3]

In sharp contrast to Bell, whose conception of significant
form was absolute and not actually amenable to demonstra-
tion by analysis of specific works, Fry, having arrived, after
twenty-five years as a critic, at the idea of form as the single,
essential element in works of visual art, was mainly concerned with specifying the nature of form in objective terms.
The idea of form as aesthetic in essence—the product of emo-

tion felt by the artist and the stimulus of emotion in the beholder—is the premise of his mature criticism. His real distinction as a critic rests on his extraordinary ability to objectify, so far as it is possible by discursive means, his remarkable sensitivity to visual forms. By means of formal analysis he was able to communicate his own visual experience and to reveal a whole realm of aesthetic experience which had hitherto been closed to the listener or reader. Those who heard Fry's lectures have testified to this revelation. Something similar can be derived from his monograph on Cézanne, which is generously illustrated.

Fry was not a creator of systems; some of his most important work was presented in occasional essays, and his general ideas were constantly being modified by his changing response to works of art and by his own progress as a painter. Consequently, it is not easy to reduce the substance of his work to a brief summary. I shall deal first with his aesthetics, which displays a fairly consistent progression toward significant form; then with his method of formal analysis, which is not actually distinct from his general aesthetics.

Fry's early work recapitulates fairly closely the transition from the nineteenth- to the twentieth-century outlook on art, which was marked by the reaction to Ruskin. In the last decades of the nineteenth century most writers on art had rejected Ruskin's excessively simplified equation of art and morals, his version of art as a direct expression of moral states. In denying the relevance of ethical or practical criteria to art, Fry was aligned with the aesthetes. But in 1901, the date of his essay on Giotto, Fry was, in one respect, closer to Ruskin than to the Whistler of the "Ten o'Clock" Lecture, which may be taken as representing the farthest swing of the pendulum away from Ruskin. The thesis of the essay may be described as humanistic; Fry's conviction that Giotto's greatness as a painter is directly proportional to the depth and accuracy of his dramatic and psychological portrayal is not unrelated to Ruskin's treatment of the Italian painters. Fry was far from believing, even at that time, that the primary function of painting was the depiction of psychological states or narrative eloquence; but his criterion of greatness was "literary" in the sense that it involved materials which were not beyond the resources of literary expression. The essay on Giotto has nothing in common with the kind of literary treatment of painting represented by Pater's celebrated pages on the "Mona Lisa." The larger part of it is devoted to formal analysis of a technical nature, to Giotto's handling of space composition, to the rhythmic organization of the figures. But these formal matters are regarded as definitely secondary to the painter's insight into the nature of human emotions. In reprinting the essay twenty years later, Fry makes an explicit recantation:

The following . . . is perhaps more than any other article here reprinted, at variance with the more recent expressions of my aesthetic ideas. It will be seen that great emphasis is laid on Giotto's expression of the dramatic idea in his pictures. I still think that this is perfectly true so far as it goes, nor do I doubt that an artist like Giotto did envisage such an expression. I should be disinclined to disagree wherever in this article there appears the assumption not only that the dramatic idea may have inspired the artist to the creation of his form, but that the value of the form for us is bound up with recognition of the dramatic idea. It now seems to me possible by a more searching analysis of our experience in front of a work of art to disentangle our reaction to pure form from our reaction to its implied associated ideas.[4]

In retracting his earlier views, there is no indication that Fry had altered his over-all judgment of Giotto. He would certainly not have subscribed to Clive Bell's view of Giotto's work as an aesthetic disaster marking the beginning of the decadence which followed the end of the Byzantine formal tradition. The essay itself is not the product of naïveté or of cultural lag, for at the time of writing it Fry was fully aware of the formalist argument.

It is true that in speaking of these [literary effects] one is led inevitably to talk of elements in the work which modern criticism is apt to regard as lying outside the domain of pictorial art. It is customary to dismiss all that concerns the dramatic presentation of the subject as literature or illustration which is to be sharply distinguished from the qualities of design. But can this clear distinction be drawn in fact? . . . The painter like Giotto . . . actually imagines in terms of figures capable of pictorial present-ment, he does not merely translate a poetically dramatic vision into pictorial terms. And to be able to do this implies a constant observation of natural forms with a bias towards the discovery of pictorial beauty. To be able, then, to conceive just the appropriate pose of a hand to express the right idea of character and emotion, is surely as much a matter of a painter's vision as to appreciate the relative "values" of a tree and cloud so as to convey the mood proper to a particular landscape.[5]

In this essay Fry raises a point which is still highly prob-lematical in art criticism: can a distinction be drawn be-tween the formal and nonformal elements in a work, and to what extent can the supposedly nonformal elements be as-similated in the formal ones? The issue has been sharpened by the emergence of nonfigurative art, whereas Fry was operating within the framework of representational art re-garded as a norm. Fry was actually engaged in a highly fruitful line of investigation—the aesthetic status of pre-sumably nonformal properties in the visual arts. There were several motives which led him to abandon it in favor of a unilateral formalism. The first of these was the lesson of modern French painting, which he was later to label as Post-Impressionist. Without having abandoned representa-tion, or more strictly speaking, figurative elements, the Post-Impressionists had increasingly subordinated them to the demands of form. The effects of this painting on Fry was

to involve him more deeply in aesthetic speculation. Formulations such as "a constant observation of natural forms with
a bias towards the discovery of pictorial beauty" were not
applicable to the new art. His aesthetics was tending toward
the position taken by Clive Bell, namely, that aesthetic experience itself was solely concerned with visual form and
therefore discontinuous with "human emotion." Fry was
strongly drawn toward the idea of the dehumanization of art;
but even after he had committed himself to an outright
formalism he was not dogmatic, and occasionally certain
echoes from the past are heard.

The idea of art as an absolute has exercised a powerful
spell upon modern art theory. Fry was strongly drawn to
the Symbolist ideal of a poetry which approached the purity
and autonomy of music, and it is not surprising that the
poetry of Mallarmé was his chief literary enthusiasm.
Whereas Clive Bell prudently exempted literature from the
aesthetics based on the idea of significant form, Fry was
beguiled by the notion of pure poetry, in which the form was
everything, the matter nothing. But Fry was rarely as radical
in his criticism of the visual arts as in his aesthetics. His
actual conception of pictorial form, far from being dehumanized, was firmly rooted in man's physical and psychological experience.

The aesthetic point of view exposed in the essay on Giotto
may be roughly described as expressionist: the painter is ultimately judged by the depth and range of human emotion
conveyed in his work. At the same time Fry is aware that
dramatic power and psychological insight are achieved by
formal means. Such elements as volume, mass, composition,
pose, and movement are employed to further the dramatic
idea. Accordingly, there is no essential discontinuity between form and matter; the fusion of both takes place in the
interest of expression. But in performing its expressive function, form may violate the canon of beauty. Discussing the

works of an inferior painter, the master of "The Deception of Isaac," which had previously been attributed to Giotto, Fry points out: "They are not dramatic and intense as Giotto's; they show a more conscious aspiration after style; the artist will not allow the requirements of formal beauty to be disturbed by the desire for expressive and life-like gestures." [6]

One can perceive that the idea of formal beauty as a definite, objective quantity in aesthetics would prove to be as much of an embarrassment in the formalist aesthetics as in the expressionist aesthetics which Fry was to abandon. In view of Fry's profoundest admirations in painting—Giotto, Rembrandt, Cézanne, and the Post-Impressionists—one can understand his relief at jettisoning the idea of beauty as the basis of aesthetics. Fry acknowledged Tolstoy's *What is Art?* as the work which delivered him from an impasse and made possible a fruitful approach to aesthetic problems. Tolstoy himself might have found it ironic that his essay should have been of crucial importance in the development of a formalist aesthetic. Fry, of course, was concerned only with the premise that communication of emotion rather than the production of beauty was the distinctive feature of art, not with the moralistic inferences that Tolstoy drew from this premise.

The "Essay on Aesthetics" (1909) marks a decisive stage in Fry's progress toward formalism. The issue is still that of morality in art; the antagonist is the Puritan tradition in British culture and intellectual life. Fry's argument is based on a rough-hewn psychology which differentiates between instinctive behavior resulting in action and imaginative behavior producing no practical consequences. In this context imagination is not employed in the Coleridgean sense of a special cognitive mode; the distinctive feature of the imaginative life for Fry consists in its contemplative and nonutilitarian character. The imagination is, first of all, free; being wholly contemplative, without resultant action, it is not subject to moral judgment. In the second place, the imagination is disinterested; it makes possible a kind of awareness of both objects and their emotional attributes, a kind of attention to them which does not exist on the level of instinctive or practical behavior. Despite his antipathy toward aestheticism, Fry verges upon the conception of art as autonomous. For the imagination produces aesthetic emotions which are not subject to ethical judgment: "Morality, then, appreciates emotion by the standard of resultant action. Art appreciates emotion in and for itself." [7]

Since the idea of detachment, of disinterestedness, was the ruling principle of Roger Fry's intellectual life, and since his aesthetics was largely empirical, founded upon his own response to works of art, it was natural, perhaps, that he should have come to view aesthetic experience itself as an activity obedient to its own laws, and art as aspiring toward a state of purity or austerity from which all impure elements have been eliminated. It was a tactical error on the part of Fry to define aesthetic experience in psychological terms, and to ascribe it to a special psychological faculty, since his doctrine was made vulnerable to attack on purely psychological grounds. Fry, no less than Clive Bell, was the object of I. A. Richards' assault on formalism. Fry's polarities of instinct and imagination, action and contemplation, were phrased in the framework of behaviorist psychology. The formalist hypothesis is better served by both Gestalt psychology and psychoanalysis, but this would involve abandonment of an autotelic aesthetics.

The separation of art and morality which is the starting point of the "Essay on Aesthetics" leaves Fry with an autonomous realm of emotion: "We must therefore give up the attempt to judge the work of art by its reaction on life, and consider it as an expression of emotions regarded as ends in themselves." [8] Emotion is at best an extremely difficult term in aesthetic discourse and Fry does not specify its meaning. Obviously it is not the sort of emotion conveyed by dramatic expression and psychological insight which Fry had admired in Giotto's work. In the present context it appears to be closely related to sensation:

If, then, an object of any kind is created by man not for use, for its fitness to actual life, but as an object of art, an object sub-serving the imaginative life, what will its qualities be? It must in the first place be adapted to that disinterested intensity of con-templation, which we found to be the effect of cutting off the responsive action. It must be suited to that heightened power of perception which we found to result therefrom. And the first quality that we demand in our sensations will be order, without which our sensations will be troubled and perplexed, and the other quality will be variety, without which they will not be fully stimulated.[9]

The precise relationship between sensation and emotion is not made evident, but it is quite clear that the emotions pertaining to art, inasmuch as they are "ends in themselves," are aroused by or connected with what we recognize as the formal elements in the visual arts, although Fry does not actually use the term in this essay. The demand for order and variety on the sensuous level is apparently transformed into emotion on the plane of contemplative perception. What Fry calls "the emotional elements of design" are precisely those formal elements we encounter in contemporary anal-yses of form—line, mass, space, light and shade, color, the disposition of planes. Fry's list is not absolutely exhaustive; he does not attach importance to surface texture and brush-work as elements of form, for instance. But I am not so much concerned with the adequacy of Fry's instrument of analysis as with its implications for his aesthetics. Fry had not yet reached the point of declaring, with Clive Bell, that aesthetic emotion is by definition unrelated to life. He is no longer concerned with dramatic emotion, to be sure, but rather with emotions involved in man's physical existence.

And these are related to life, if only on the level of sensation and perception. Fry admits that the emotional effect of any one of these formal elements is very weak when abstracted from the whole and reduced to diagrammatic terms. But when combined with the representation of natural appearances—above all, with the appearance of the human body—the effect is enormously heightened. It is not clear whether Fry, at this point, regards representation as absolutely essential in the production of aesthetic emotion, but he is not yet prepared to discard it. Furthermore, he has not yet exorcised the ghost of naturalism. Having been derived from natural forms, the "emotional elements of design" in these forms are capable of inducing an aesthetic effect; what natural forms lack is the purposive quality of artistic production:

> Nature is heartlessly indifferent to the needs of the imaginative life . . . We have no guarantee that in nature the emotional elements will be combined appropriately with the demands of the imaginative life, and it is, I think, the great occupation of the graphic arts to give us first of all order and variety in the sensuous plane and then so to arrange the sensuous presentment of objects that the emotional elements are elicited with an order and appropriateness altogether beyond what Nature herself provides.[10]

In linking the elements of design with certain fundamental physical and physiological experiences, Fry was undoubtedly influenced by the aesthetics of empathy and pure visibility. His views have a certain relationship to those of Hildebrand's *The Problem of Form in Figurative Art* (1893); the "emotional elements of design" are not dissimilar to Bernard Berenson's "ideated sensations." But the idea of form is not yet crystallized; it contains an unresolved and unexplained duality. On the one hand, pictorial form would appear to consist of sensuous elements which when combined demonstrate certain qualities of order susceptible of geometrical analysis such as unity and balance, and others which are nongeometrical—certain sequences in which "each successive element is felt to have a fundamental and harmonious relationship with that which preceded it." [11] But on the other hand, Fry is unable to show how aesthetic emotion is related to sensuous design, how the emotions themselves are ordered.

It was Clive Bell's bold hypothesis of significant form together with the more experimental features of Post-Impressionist painting, such as Cubism, which enabled Fry to resolve these difficulties, but it was a resolution achieved at the price of an even wider separation of art and life and a more severe and limited conception of form as "pure, abstract design." In the essay entitled "Retrospect" (1920), Fry traced the further development of his aesthetic ideas and clarified some of the ambiguities present in "An Essay on Aesthetics." Having abandoned beauty as the prime aesthetic criterion and having adopted a quasi-expressionist view "I conceived the form of the work of art to be its most essential quality, but I believed this form to be the direct outcome of an apprehension of some emotion of actual life by the artist . . . I conceived the form and the emotion which it conveyed as being inextricably bound together in the aesthetic whole." [12] It was apparently the direct testimony of certain contemporary artists who were extraordinarily sensitive to form and formal relations that led Fry to modify his view of form as an expression of emotion. Profoundly moved by form, these men were not aware of those emotions of "actual life" which Fry had presumed to be conveyed by the formal properties of their works. Since it was impossible to doubt the authenticity of their aesthetic reactions, Fry concluded that he had not yet carried formal analysis far enough nor succeeded in disentangling the purely aesthetic properties of visual art from certain residual accompaniments and associations. Clive Bell's *Art* had propounded a theory of virtually absolute aesthetic autonomy, of aesthetic experience as totally unrelated to any other kind of experience, and it seemed to Fry that this attempt to isolate "the pure aesthetic reaction from the compounds in which it occurs" was the most important single step in practical aesthetics.

The most problematic aspect of formalist aesthetics is the matter of expression, of meaning. Fry is no more successful than Bell in explaining the significance of significant form:

> I think we are all agreed that we mean by significant form something other than agreeable arrangements of form, harmonious patterns, and the like. We feel that a work which possesses it is the outcome of an endeavour to express an idea rather than to create a pleasing object. Personally, at least, I always feel that it implies an effort on the part of the artist to bend to our emotional understanding by means of his passionate conviction some intractable material which is alien to our spirit. I seem unable at present to get beyond this vague adumbration of the nature of significant form.[13]

Fry did not ever pursue the metaphysical implications of this statement. His apparently intuitive awareness of a mode of reality lying beyond the world of appearances which is made accessible by aesthetic experience has been corroborated by others, notably by certain contemporary abstract artists, but it is dubious that a metaphysical rationale of significant form would have contributed anything to Fry's "practical aesthetics," much less to his criticism.

The full import of the cognitive value of aesthetic experience would have involved Fry in consideration of form as symbol, a line of inquiry he had no desire to pursue. He had by this time recognized that his earlier aesthetic views had been vitiated by a false distinction between form and content, and he welcomed an hypothesis which staked everything on form conceived of as pure essence purged of all adventitious matter. The doctrine of significant form was

not easy to defend on logical grounds, nor did it fully account for the evidence supplied by Fry's native sensibility
to works of art, but his temporary commitment to it was not
arbitrary. It was elicited by the emergence in the twentieth
century of an art which tended toward pure form. Fry realized, of course, that ideally the formalist hypothesis should
apply not only to Post-Impressionist painting but also to the
art of all kinds in all periods. Having posited the existence
of pure form, he was confronted with the fact that the
greater part of the world's art contained impure elements.
The critic's primary task, then, would be to discriminate between the pure and impure elements. The problem of the
relationship between pure and impure, aesthetic and nonaesthetic, formal and nonformal still remained. The precise
question is whether there can be a true union of the aesthetic
and nonaesthetic:

Probably at this point we must hand over the question to the
experimental psychologist. It is for him to discover whether this
fusion is possible, whether, for example, such a thing as a song
really exists, that is to say, a song in which neither the meaning
of the words nor the meaning of the music predominates; in
which music and words do not merely set up separate currents
of feeling, but really fuse and become indivisible. I expect that
the answer will be negative. If on the other hand such a complete
fusion of different kinds of emotion does take place, this would
tend to substantiate the ordinary opinion that aesthetic emotion
has greater value in highly complicated compounds than in the
pure state.[14]

Fry was to settle the problem for himself in an essay
titled "Some Questions in Aesthetics" (1926), not, to be sure,
by experimental means, but by a combination of introspection and formal analysis. Under the tutelage of modern art,
he was able to perceive in himself a separation of aesthetic
and nonaesthetic emotion which corresponded with the formal and nonformal elements in the work itself. By this time

he had modified his conception of form as rooted in certain fundamental psycho-physical experiences into one of the visual form as severely abstract, stripped almost entirely of sensuous content. The occasion of this essay, though perhaps not its actual motive, was I. A. Richards' devastating treatment of significant form and the concomitant idea of distinctively aesthetic emotion in *The Principles of Criticism* (1924). The issue is whether aesthetic and nonaesthetic experience coöperate (in Richards' phrase), whether they form a true compound (in Fry's). Richards is undoubtedly on firmer psychological ground than Fry, but his evidence is drawn mainly from literature, an art which is much more recalcitrant to formalism than the visual arts. The argument, as Fry conducts it, centers on the nature of the relationship of representation and form in painting, which he takes to correspond with the relationship of content and form in poetry; his general conclusion is that representation and form do not actually achieve a true compound or fusion and that representation, as Clive Bell maintained, was irrelevant to the purely aesthetic effect. Fry appears to have subscribed to Pater's dictum that all the arts aspire toward the condition of music, and to have arrived at the view that form in its most characteristic state is to be found in "certain peculiarly abstract musical constructions or even of certain kinds of architecture," that is, in nonrepresentational art which is also at the farthest possible remove from ordinary human experience. The sensuous basis of pictorial form is discarded in favor of what Sir Kenneth Clark has called an almost Pythagorean conception. Aesthetic emotion is derived not so much from the sensuous elements of painting themselves—line, mass, space, light and shade, color—as from the relationship of these elements.

Now the crucial fact which appears to me to arise from the comparison of a number of these experiences which are the subject of our inquiry is that in all cases our reaction to works of art is a

reaction to a relation and not to sensations or objects or persons
or events. This, if I am right, affords a distinguishing mark of
what I call esthetic experience, esthetic reactions, or esthetic
states of mind.[15]

Without actually repudiating the idea of aesthetic emotion,
Fry here definitely tends toward a more intellectualized approach to art which is reflected in the phrase "esthetic states
of mind."

Fry does not argue for a special mental faculty to account
for these states of mind, but he feels that there is "a constant
and recognisable pattern of the mental disposition, in such
situations." The closest analogy outside the arts is the mental
state of the pure mathematician. In this particular essay Fry
is not concerned either with a precise description of the nature of formal relations in painting or with their classification. Indeed, he is highly aware of the extreme difficulty, if
not impossibility, of reducing to verbal discourse the quality
of these relations, and is compelled to fall back on analogy.
The sense of inevitability induced by certain formal structures, for instance, is compared with the structure of tragedy:

It became evident to me that the essential of great tragedy was
not the emotional intensity of the events portrayed, but the vivid
sense of the inevitability of their unfolding, the significance of the
curve of crescendo and diminuendo which their sequence describes, together with all the myriad subsidiary evocations which,
at each point, poetic language can bring in to give fullness and
density to the whole organic unity.[16]

In the realm of painting this kind of structure is perceived
in certain spatial constructions, in which volumes are related
to each other by means of plastic relief. Plastic forms are
seen by Fry as a kind of musicalized geometry in which the
plastic elements are grouped in a rhythmic sequence, a
movement which culminates in a harmonious whole.

In order to refute Richards' assertion that formal and representational elements in painting combine to form a unified aesthetic experience, Fry undertakes the detailed analyses of a series of four works—Breughel's "Carrying of the Cross," Daumier's "Gare St. Lazare," Poussin's "Ulysses," and Rembrandt's "Christ Before Pilate"—ranged in an ascending order of plastic fulfillment and spatial construction. Fry is very successful in demonstrating that the representation of what we may call "literary" subject matter has very little bearing on what he discovers to be the formal relations in each of these works. Of the Poussin, in which the subject matter is largely conventional and not compelling in treatment he says:

How unexpectedly, how deliciously right is our ejaculation as we turn from one detail to another or as we contemplate the mutual relations of the main volumes to the whole space. And this contemplation arouses in us a very definite mood . . . which . . . has nothing whatever to do with psychological entities . . . as remote from any emotions suggested by the subject, as it would be if I listened to one of Bach's fugues.[17]

The Rembrandt is a different matter, for here the subject is of compelling interest. But even in a work in which the gift for illustration and the gift for plastic construction are equally great, Fry finds it impossible to focus on both form and subject matter simultaneously: "We are compelled to focus the two elements separately . . . How can we keep the attention fixed on the spaceless world of psychological entities and upon the apprehension of spatial relations? . . . We constantly shift our attention backwards and forwards from one to another." [18]

Quite apart from the whole question of visual forms as a symbolic language capable of expressing psychic states which reveal the apprehension of an inner or outer reality, Fry would appear to have won his point on what might be called nineteenth-century terms. He conclusively proves the irrelevance of likeness or verisimilitude, as well as that of subject matter, to aesthetic experience. The final stage of his argument concerns Corot's "View of Honfleur," an example of realism devoid of the literary or psychological content which were prominent in the four works previously dealt with. Realism is a highly ambiguous term, but in this context it may be taken to signify the plain transcription of given visual data uninformed by the need or desire to idealize them:

The plain matter-of-fact was accepted without protest, rather, indeed with a certain avidity, for to Corot's eye these simple appearances yielded one of those mysteriously perfect chords of colour in which every note gets a new meaning and resonance, and at the same time helps to create a plastic unity of the space with all its content of air and light. And that harmony is found by such subtle, infinitesimal and unconscious adjustments of the ordinary accepted facts of appearance that to one who missed Corot's real meaning it would have the non-aesthetic meaning, such as it is, of an exact reproduction of the scene. What concerns us here is that the realism, complete as it is, is so entirely transmuted into plastic values that to say before it, "How like Honfleur!" would be felt to be totally irrelevant to the mood it evokes —a mood as detached from any actual experience as that of the purest music. In short, Corot creates here an entirely spiritual reality.[19]

By invoking the idea of spiritual reality, Fry is far from assigning a symbolic function to visual forms. As a matter of fact he implies the contrary notion that these forms are necessarily nonreferential and autonomous:

We can say, supposing the picture to envisage plastic expression, that the moment anything in it ceases to serve towards the identification of the whole plastic volume, the moment it depends on reference to something outside the picture, it becomes descriptive of some other reality, and becomes a part of an actual, and not spiritual reality.[20]

At this precise point Fry reached the ultimate stage in the development of a formalist aesthetics. Ideally, the work of art is conceived of as being self-sufficient, self-contained, and self-explanatory. The next logical step would have been to advocate an art of pure form, that is, nonobjective art. But while Fry did not regard the idea of nonobjective art as untenable from a theoretical standpoint, he was not to become one of its prophets. His notion of the autonomy of aesthetic experience was arrived at by a negative process, so to speak, by the successive elimination of nonessential elements— first, subject matter conceived of as illustration, then the depiction of psychological states, and finally representation itself, the transcription of visual data. What we are left with is form conceived of as the relationship within the picture of specifically pictorial elements which do have a representational function.

The controlling factor in Fry's conception of those autonomous formal relations which constitute the aesthetic substance of the work of art is the idea of plasticity, the representation of three-dimensional space on a two-dimensional surface. Fry's skill in formal analysis depended in large part on an acute sense of plastic values. His dismissal of a two-dimensional treatment of the picture plane as decorative rather than aesthetically significant is founded on a profoundly personal bias: "It is doubtful whether a purely flat surface, without suggestions of significant volume, can arouse any profound emotion. . . ." [21] Fry's sense of form is by no means eccentric or arbitrary; it is corroborated by the history of European painting up to and including Cézanne. But its limitations have been made apparent by the phenomenon of nonobjective art. In the last analysis, Fry does not accept the idea of an absolutely autonomous art; for, if almost all of the significant formal elements in painting compose an internal and intrinsic "spiritual" reality having no reference to the external world, nevertheless the elements taken singly are derived from our awareness of the physical universe. Fry said of the "Portrait of Mme. Cézanne": "It belongs to a world of spiritual values incommensurate with but parallel with the actual world." [22] Despite Fry's conviction that aesthetic experience constitutes an awareness of spiritual reality, Sir Herbert Read has found Fry's conception of art to be excessively materialistic in that it is based on the requirement of plastic form.

The primary flaw in Clive Bell's aesthetics, as we have seen, was his inability to account for the presence of significant form in a work of art except in terms of a purely subjective reaction which could be identified by its intensity, first of all, and qualitatively by its uniqueness, its total difference from all other kinds of emotion. Fry's pronouncements on form in art may ultimately be traced to a reaction no less subjective; but his intellectual endowments and his scientific training led him to make a determined effort to disentangle the work as object from his own reactions, to analyze and explain its structure in terms that are meaningful to other viewers. Perhaps criticism can go no farther than this. If we are led to conclude that Fry's generalizations concerning art were rationalizations of his own intuitive preferences, his theory of art is nevertheless preferable to an eclecticism which fails to reflect the product of sensibility, of intensely felt personal experience. Fry's natural tendency was to regard his conception of form as universal; the antidote would have been a historical detachment which might have lent his theory greater scope and validity but which would undoubtedly have diluted his powers as a critic. As a matter of fact, Fry's theories were not inflexible. In his last work, an unfinished series of lectures delivered during his tenure of the Slade Professorship at Cambridge University, Fry set himself the task of an historical survey of art ranging far beyond the bounds of European painting, for which his conception of form, which he had arrived at after many decades, no longer served. In these

*Last Lectures* we can perceive a modification of his views, which might have resulted, had he lived, in a theory of more universal applicability.

The theory on which Fry's accomplishment as a critic of painting is based may be summarized as follows: The source of aesthetic emotion is connected solely with a certain kind of form which we may designate as plastic. Plastic form is achieved by the transformation of the data of appearance into a unified, coherent structure, whose elements are the relations of volumes in space. The principles by which the structures themselves are ordered are autonomous, in the sense that they are peculiar to works of art. They are not imposed by a reality external to the works themselves. For Fry, these structures constitute a spiritual reality, the existence of which is attested by the emotions they invoke. While he is certain about their emotional effect, he is actually at a loss to explain the capacity of form to produce these emotions. One hypothesis is the almost perfect accord between the contemplative quality of aesthetic experience, which makes possible a concentration of attention not ordinarily experienced, and the abstract nature of formal relations.

Although Fry's theory does not dispense with the subjective element in aesthetic experience, the emphasis is shifted from the emotional impact of form to form as an intellectually apprehensible and therefore objective structure. In a relatively early statement (*Architectural Heresies of a Painter,* 1921) the approach is psychological or even physiological: "Certain relations of solid shapes to each other do set up in the mind which contemplates them a peculiar condition of tension and equilibrium, which is the essence of aesthetic emotion. And an object which has these relations that are satisfactory to aesthetic contemplation may be said to have plastic form." [23] In his later criticism he is mainly concerned with structural relations as harmonious wholes. Fry's taste was conditioned to a considerable extent by a predisposition toward clarity and rationality, insofar as these qualities can be conveyed by visual means. He was insensitive to visual configurations which, lacking these properties, nevertheless evoke emotion of a different order. Insofar as order and rationality are the properties of classical art, Fry had classical tastes; however, he was not drawn toward Graeco-Roman art, which he found wanting in plasticity, but rather to the architectonic qualities of Italian Renaissance painting which were perpetuated chiefly in French painting.

Since Fry's ideas concerning the formal properties of art were not the result of a priori thinking but of his response to actual works, they are expressed more concretely in his criticism than in his theoretical essays. As one might expect, Fry is at his best in dealing with painters for whom he had the greatest affinity, first and foremost with Cézanne, with Chardin, Claude, and Poussin, with Courbet and Manet, but not, despite their almost overwhelming appeal in this century, with the Impressionists. Fry is aware of Cézanne's debt to Impressionist techniques, a method calculated to transcribe "the marvellous territory of external vision," but he views Cézanne's formal achievement as radically opposed to the aims of Impressionism. It is highly significant that Fry attributes Cézanne's greatness to intellectual power. Although Cézanne may have appeared to be exceedingly simple-minded in most respects, for Fry he is a great intellect in respect to his single passion for form. In contrast with the Impressionists who, in Fry's judgment, were concerned with seizing the fullness and variety of surface appearances with unprecedented skill, Cézanne

saw always, however dimly, behind this veil an architecture and a logic which appealed to his most intimate feelings. Reality, no doubt, lay always behind this veil of colour, but it was different, more solid, more dense, in closer relation to the needs of the spirit. . . . He gave himself up entirely to this desperate search for the reality hidden behind the veil of appearances. . . . It is precisely this which gives to all his utterances in form tremendous, almost prophetic significance.[24]

Long before he became aware of Cézanne's epochal importance, Fry had been expert in perceiving and demonstrating formal relations and structure in painting, even though he had originally regarded them as serving expressive rather than purely formal ends. But it was primarily the work of Cézanne, particularly as it had been understood and used by the Post-Impressionists in the early years of this century, which provided the final revelation of both the nature and the significance of form. In the light of this insight, Fry was to reëvaluate the art of the past and of the present. His receptivity to modern art did not extend beyond the Post-Impressionists, and even within these limits he was mainly drawn to work whose form exhibited architectural and logical qualities. This bias toward rationality can be traced directly to his interpretation of Cézanne:

By the true Impressionist, by men like . . . Guillaumin and Pissarro, those changes of colours which correspond to movements of planes were vigorously expressed, but they were more concerned to seize the full complexity of the coloured mosaic of vision than to isolate and emphasize these indications in the total complex which are evocative of plastic form. They sought to weave across their canvas the unbroken weft of colour which their eyes had learned to perceive in nature. But this aim could not altogether satisfy such a nature as Cézanne's. The intellect is bound to seek for articulations. In order to handle nature's continuity it has to be conceived as discontinuous; without organization, without articulation, the intellect gets no leverage. And with Cézanne the intellect—or, to be more exact, the intellectual part of his sensual reactions—claimed its full rights.[25]

The search for plastic form is endowed by Fry with a quasi-ethical value, corresponding to the scientist's search for truth. Insights such as these served to reinforce the native austerity of Fry's temperament. He became increasingly suspicious of technical virtuosity, of surface charm particularly as exemplified in the marvelous texture of Impressionist painting, of emotive expression. Fry's particular brand of classicism induced in him a virtually blanket distrust of romantic painting, including Delacroix and Turner. According to Sir Kenneth Clark, he sometimes displayed an almost perverse preference for the prosaic. Fry's classicism, of course, had very little to do with the subject matter of neo-classic painting. This is made evident in his treatment of Poussin, whom he regards as the true precursor of Cézanne. He finds Poussin's subjects to be thoroughly artificial, insipid, and uninteresting. But Poussin's choice of subjects turns out to be an advantage, for it leaves us free to concentrate on the form: "Once he got to work his intense feeling for formal harmonies became his chief occupation, as indeed it remains for us, now that we no longer respond to the rhetoric of Poussin's time, the real meaning of his work . . . the endless variety and daring originality of his pictorial architecture." [26]

Fry was fond of quoting Michelangelo's statement: "Finally, good painting is a music and a melody which intellect only can appreciate." The illumination derived from Cézanne's forms did not, as was the case with Clive Bell, require a radical revision of Fry's attitude toward the art of the Italian Renaissance, but actually confirmed his earliest admirations. He had always been indifferent to the Venetians, whom Ruskin had preferred above all other Italian painters, and who have always ranked high with those who value their painterly quality. Fry had always been more strongly drawn toward the architectonic painting of the Florentines, and the opening paragraph of his essay on "The Art of Florence" (1919) reveals the basis of his preference:

The idea of the artist as the plaything of whim and caprice, a hypersensitive and incoherent emotionalist is, no doubt, true of a certain class of men, many of whom practice the arts; nothing could be further from a true account of those artists whose work has had the deepest influence on the tradition of art; nothing could be less true of the great artists of the Florentine School. From the rise of modern art in the thirteenth century till now Florence and France have been the decisive factors in the art of Europe. Without them our art might have reflected innumerable pathetic or dramatic moods, it might have illustrated various curious or moving situations, it would not have attained to the conception of generalized truth of form. To Florence of the fourteenth and fifteenth centuries and to France of the seventeenth and succeeding centuries we owe the creation of generalized or what, for want of a better word, we may call "intellectual" art.[27]

Fry refers, we may observe, to "the tradition of art" in the singular. Just as the classical tradition itself, which emerged in the Renaissance and dominated European conceptions of art until the end of the eighteenth century, had at its core a belief in the universality of the canon of beauty derived from Graeco-Roman sculpture, Fry tends also to confer universal value on his own conception of form which is derived from a single European tradition. The tendency is much more common in the field of aesthetics and art criticism than is its opposite, pluralism or relativism. Fry abhorred dogmatism and guarded himself against a narrow view of art, but in spite of these scruples, he was incapable of a wholehearted appreciation of a large and important segment of European art—Northern as distinguished from Mediterranean art. He finds Flemish art, for all its astonishing skill in the imitation of familiar things, to be deficient in that which matters, "the universal aspects of form," and he attributes its failure to its inheritance of the tradition of Gothic design, a decorative rather than a formal art.

Not only is Fry's conception of plastic form bound up with a single tradition but also primarily with a single branch of the visual arts—painting. One of the distinguishing features of Florentine painting in the fourteenth century is its integral relationship with the arts of sculpture and architecture. This resulted in a new sense of the disposition on a flat surface of volumes and masses in space. The transformation of three-dimensional data in two-dimensional terms provides painting with those intellectual attributes which can be dealt with by Fry's categories of harmony, logic, coherence, inevitability. At one point in his speculations, he actually perceived the problem of form in painting as a polar tension between two-dimensional and three-dimensional effects, between the linear and the plastic. He is discussing line drawings, specifically the "rhythmic flow of line" which may be interpreted as the personal gesture of a signature of the artist:

[The] calligraphic quality tends to divert our attention from the cross section of disappearing planes and fixes it on the continuous movement of their summation in line. It is one aspect of the eternal conflict in the graphic arts of the organisation of the surface of the picture and its organisation as an ideated three-dimensional space occupied by volumes. The conciliation of these two opposing tendencies, accomplished by innumerable different devices at different periods, may almost be said to be the material of any intimate technical criticism of pictorial art.[28]

Fry's aesthetics as applied in his criticism is adapted primarily to the elucidation of pictorial art and is most successful in dealing with painting which adheres to the tradition of plastic form. I have concentrated on the central aspect of Fry's work and have necessarily given a highly restricted view of his over-all capacities as a critic. Reference has been made to his indifference to texture in painting; while it is true that he did not regard it as relevant to form, he was extraordinarily aware of surface texture in sculpture as a manifestation of style. And although he was inclined to view calligraphy as essentially decorative, he possessed a rare sensitivity to linear rhythms in all the arts. It would appear that, by means of a self-imposed discipline, he rejected the aesthetic significance of all evidence of personal expression in art.

As previously indicated, the Cambridge lectures given by Fry in the last year of his life reveal certain modifications of what I have called his central doctrine which, if more fully developed, might have constituted a major revision of the formalist aesthetics. His approach was chronological, beginning with Egyptian art. Up to the point at which they break off—late Greek, Hellenistic, and Roman art—the lectures deal almost exclusively with sculpture, to which the concept of plastic form as "ideated three-dimensional space" does not apply. The point of view is formalist to the extent that Fry still regards as irrelevant to criticism all information conveyed by the work which cannot be apprehended in purely visual terms. But the idea of form is expanded to include properties other than plasticity. The key terms are sensibility and vitality; they reflect an entirely new phase in Fry's speculations on art, motivated by an interest in psychoanalysis and by the possibility that visual forms are intimately connected with the unconscious. Fry does not abandon the idea of art as a contemplative activity, autonomous in the sense that it is wholly independent of nonartistic activity, but we can detect a greater emphasis on visual forms as directly related to affective states. He makes a larger allowance for personality as a factor in style and no longer appears to view artistic production as an impersonal, abstruse process:

The artist is then a man who has experiences of one kind or another which excite him in such a way that first of all for his own satisfaction he wishes to hold them in the focus of attention until he has exactly appreciated their quality, and this holding in focus results in the work of art, poem, picture or what not . . . With the artist certain experiences have the power to arrest his attention so much that he turns aside from the current of life and waits until he has fixed that experience fully in his consciousness and extracted its full savour . . . With the [visual] artist it is almost always primarily a visual experience, although it is possible that an experience of a non-visual kind my be projected outwards in visible forms . . . [The] experience [is] composed of two elements: one, the situation, the external stimulus, which in the case of art we may generally identify with the subject of the picture, and on the other the whole nature of the artist which causes his reaction to that stimulus to be just what it is . . . No two artists subjected to the same outward stimulus can possibly produce identical works of art.[29]

In the past, Fry had scrupulously avoided the genetic approach in criticism. Since virtually all of the works illustrated and discussed in these lectures are anonymous, there is no way of knowing how far Fry was willing to carry his new insight. But it is unlikely that he would have attempted to convert the hypothesis of psychological causality into a critical device, since the role of the unconscious is highly obscure:

What the artist brings to the particular experience is much more than his immediate consciousness of it. His reaction is coloured by all sorts of subconscious associations and feelings . . . which affect profoundly the form taken by the work of art and which have the power to stir up corresponding subconscious feelings in the spectator. It is this fact . . . that gives it its peculiar, and as we say "magic" power over us. It is magic because the effect on our feelings often far transcends what we can explain by our conscious experience.[30]

In this new orientation of Fry's thought, what is the role of plastic form, of the quasi-intellectual structures, which Fry had for so long regarded as the essential element in aesthetic experience? It still occupies a central position: "The emotions evoked by the actual texture and substance of the picture . . . depend upon mastery of the specific idiom of pictorial design, recognition of the perfect coherence of complex elements in a total unity."[31] But where his aesthetics had previously excluded nearly everything but pure abstract design, he is now interested in the subtle modifications of form brought about by the medium and by the executant, visible in the surface texture of the work. It is evident that these modifications are somehow related to the total formal unity, but it is not clear whether they are actually integral. He refers on the one hand to "the feeling expressed in the design, in the planning and proportion of the parts to the whole," and on the other to the feeling expressed by an artist in executing the design. The first relates to plastic form, the second to what Fry calls sensibility, the material, sensuous quality of art as distinguished from the abstract, intellectual aspects of form.

Fry was fond of dualistic formulations, as seen in his division of experience into the practical and the contemplative, and in the polarity of the linear and plastic. Reverting to an idea which had occurred rather early in his writings, he now perceives art as a tension and balance between the principle of order and that of variety:

Design—corresponds with our desire to find order in things, our sense of immutable law and causation; sensibility—corresponds to our desire for variety, multiplicity, chance, the unforeseeable. We may say that the conscious mind tends to a mechanistic view of things, a view amenable to mathematical statement; the unconscious brings in the vital element which eludes mathematical statement. . . . In works of art [there is] a compromise between the mathematical order in which the intellect finds satisfaction and the conformity to type, but with the infinite variation which distinguishes organic life. In art there is at once order and uniqueness, which means incessant variation from the precise or mathematical order. And this precisely is the cause of what I shall boldly call the intellectual pleasure in art.[32]

It seems to me that this schematization of visual form, in which one part is assigned to the intellect, the other to the unconscious, raises more difficulties than it solves. But if it is an imperfect hypothesis, it does nevertheless reflect a

broadening of Fry's theoretical views in order to cope with
kinds of art which lie outside the European tradition—with
Scythian metalwork and with African sculpture, for example. In addition to sensibility, in the special sense employed by Fry, he introduces another criterion of value—that
of vitality. He is not able to define vitality accurately, but
it would appear to be similar to the notion of organic form,
which we usually associate with romantic rather than classical aesthetics. Fry assigns the highest degree of importance
to vitality as a quality of sculpture; it is the basis for his low
estimate of Greek sculpture of all periods and for his great
admiration of certain kinds of primitive art. Vitality is almost entirely a formal phenomenon, having very little to
do with likeness. As a matter of fact, the power of an image
to communicate the sense of an inner life is probably in in-
verse proportion to representational completeness. It is usually achieved by a suppression of all aspects of a figure which
do not actually contribute to its effect. Vitality and sensibility
are not identical, the former referring to the formal properties of figures, the latter to execution and surface; but they
are closely linked, one appearing in conjunction with the
other. In the following reference to Chinese bronzes they
appear to be virtually interchangeable:

These bronzes will illustrate the peculiar aesthetic quality of
Chou art: the rigorous coordination of the parts in a single unity
and the full sensibility of the handling. It is this tense equilibrium
between sensibility and controlling intelligence which is so
fascinating to us. I find the essentials of plastic harmony in almost
their purest, most elemental expression in these bronzes . . . It
is this peculiar tension between controlling intelligence which
establishes unified structural design, and the free vital rhythms
which belong to our unconscious gestures which gives to Chou
art its almost mysterious evocative power.[33]

I think it significant that Fry avoids the term *form,* using
*design* in its place, and that he reserves his highest praise for

work which shows a conjunction of design, on the one hand, and of sensibility and vitality, on the other. The strict formalist hypothesis of "Some Questions in Aesthetics" (1926) would appear to be inadequate to account for certain expressive features of primitive and exotic art which provoked in him powerful aesthetic reactions. But we would not be justified therefore in regarding this last phase of Fry's criticism as a conversion to a romantic-expressionist aesthetics. His point of view remained eminently classical, for sensibility and vitality are valued not in and for themselves but only as adjuncts of forms distinguished by rationality and order. He retained to the end a profound aversion for art which is deliberately employed as the vehicle of personal emotion. He asks himself whether he can find vitality in a work which he considers to be actually bad (that is, aesthetically unsatisfactory) and concludes that almost all works in this category fall under the heading of Expressionism: "Expressionism is almost as marked a peculiarity of German art as Beauty . . . is of Greek . . . The artist tries not only to realize his idea but to express to the world his feeling about his idea. In effect the artist comes out from his work . . . and nudges our elbow." [34]

Fry is thinking primarily of an artist like Grünewald. Although he may have known the work of the twentieth-century German Expressionists, he does not, to my knowledge, discuss them in his writings. But his attitude toward them may be inferred from his views on Van Gogh, who of the French Post-Impressionists is closest to the aims of Expressionism. In an essay on Van Gogh reprinted in *Transformations* (1926), Fry pays full tribute to the man, to the intensity of his convictions and his saintlike devotion to his craft, but he has serious reservations about his art. He perceives that the intensity of Van Gogh's feeling endowed his hand with certainty and rhythm, with what Fry was later to identify as sensibility and vitality. He recognizes Van Gogh's extraor-

dinary sensitiveness to color. But these are relatively minor
virtues compared with what Fry held to be the possession
of the true artist—that highly specialized reaction to visual
phenomena which results in plastic form. The real theme of
Van Gogh's art is the "agitation of his own mental states."
Of one of his greatest works, the "Cornfield with Rooks,"
Fry says:

The dramatic feeling outweighs all other considerations. There
is no longer any heed given to questions of formal design, and
Van Gogh ends, as one might have guessed from his temperament that he must end, as an inspired illustrator . . . Perhaps
after all it would be truer to say that all along he was much more
an illustrator than a plastic artist.[35]

Fry concludes with an estimate of Van Gogh's historical position:

To tell the truth, his work visibly declines in importance. He
was the exact opposite of those artists like the early Corot, Sisley,
and Seurat, whose work continues gradually to unfold the full
richness of feeling hidden beneath its superficial unimpressive-
ness some decades after the artist's death. Van Gogh staked all on
the first shock of his attack, and as we recover from that we look
in vain for further revelations. Certainly he was a more remarkable man than he was an artist.[36]

Mainly because of his inability to respond to formal properties in painting which did not contribute to the classic conception of design, Fry failed to perceive Van Gogh's expressionist approach as a formal achievement which was destined
to have an enormous influence on twentieth-century painting
quite apart from its illustrative values. Fry would have been
perplexed by the extraordinary success of expressionist painting in our own time, particularly of Abstract Expressionism,
which dispenses with the dramatic and illustrative content to
which one might ascribe the popular appeal of Van Gogh.

Fry had always been convinced that the specialized vision of the artist was intrinsically remote from ordinary human experience, and that the number of people who were capable of reacting to that vision was necessarily limited, since few could arrive at the contemplative, detached state necessary to both the conception and appreciation of aesthetic forms. The massive public resistance to the art of Cézanne and Post-Impressionists, which Fry encountered in 1910, only served to confirm this belief. What Fry did not foresee at that time was the full extent of the revolution in taste which he himself had helped to initiate. The next fifty years were to bring about not only the almost universal recognition of the modern art of which he was the champion, but a receptivity to formal experimentation far in excess of his own tastes.

Fry now appears to have been excessively cautious, excessively limited by his traditionalism. One could compose a long list of his deficiencies—his indifference to the linear tradition of Northern art, his prejudice against Expressionism and against German art in general, his bias against the French and German romantic schools, his lack of interest in technical experiment, and finally his failure to perceive the significance of nonobjective art. But all these shortcomings are more than outweighed by his positive achievements. Among contemporary critics, none has surpassed him in devotion to the visual arts as a subject worthy of the most serious intellectual consideration. His skill and precision in conveying to his listeners and readers his own grasp of the formal significance of individual works have remained unequaled. He succeeded where his formalist predecessors had failed, in providing an objective framework for the formal analysis of art. Since Fry was combating during a large part of his career the prevailing attitude toward painting which placed primary stress on its illustrative content and its literary associations, he tended toward the opposite extreme—an aestheticism which isolated art from human experience. He did succeed in establishing, if not the idea of the autonomy of form, that of the primacy of form in the fruitful investigation of visual art.

# HERBERT READ

1893  Born December 4, eldest son of Herbert Read of Muscoates Grange, Kirbymoorside, Yorkshire, a farmer, descendant of a long line of Yorkshire farmers. Read spent his first ten years on this relatively isolated farm. He has written a detailed, sensitive account of his childhood in *The Innocent Eye,* an intellectual autobiography. Read received his earliest education from a series of governesses.

1904  Death of father. Read was sent to a school for orphans in Halifax, near Manchester.

1908  Joined his mother in Leeds. Served for three years as a clerk in a local savings bank. Attended night school, but was mainly self-educated during this period. Wished first to become a doctor; decided later to enter the profession of law.

1910  Discovered poetry. His literary education was furthered by friendship with a tailor, who was also named Read and who possessed a considerable library. Discovered the work of Ibsen, Turgenev, Dostoevsky, Chekhov. Began to write verse. First poetic model was Tennyson. Discovered Blake, who made a tremendous and lasting impression on him. Admired the poems of Ralph Hodgson.

1912  Matriculated in the University of Leeds, where he pursued work toward a double degree in literature and in political

143

economy. Discovered Nietzsche, Schopenhauer, Kant, Hegel, Hume, Pascal, Plato. Received encouragement as a poet from F. W. Moorman, professor of English literature. Read Henry James, Flaubert, Rimbaud, Baudelaire.

1915 Joined Army in January. Received commission in the Green Howards, the regiment of the North Riding of Yorkshire. A volume of his verse was published at his own expense by Elkin Matthews, London. Became interested in Imagist poetry. Adopted as his poetic creed the Preface to *Some Imagist Poets: An Anthology* (1915). Published Imagist poems in *Gryphon,* students' magazine in Leeds.

1915– Spent three years at the front in Belgium and France.
1918  Decorated with Military Cross and Distinguished Service Order. During leaves, he formed acquaintance with F. S. Flint, Richard Aldington, Ezra Pound, T. S. Eliot, A. R. Orage, Wyndham Lewis.

1916 Published *Fables from Flanders,* short prose sketches.

1917 Also during leave, founded *Art and Letters,* a literary review, with Frank Ritter, director of the City Art Gallery, Leeds, who managed the magazine. The review reproduced drawings by Walter Sickert, Lucien Pissarro, McKnight Kauffer. It appeared until spring, 1920.

1918 His "Definitions Towards a Modern Theory of Poetry" published in *Art and Letters.* Published articles on syndicalism and guild socialism. Met Ford Madox Ford, who encouraged him in his ambition to become a novelist.

1919 Left army. Entered the Civil Service as Assistant Principal in the Treasury. Published *Naked Warriors,* a volume of war poems; *Eclogues,* a volume of verse.

1922   Resigned from Treasury to become Assistant Keeper, Department of Ceramics, Victoria and Albert Museum; held this position for ten years.

1923   *Mutation of the Phoenix,* poems.

1924   *The Retreat,* a prose account of the retreat of the Fifth Army from Saint-Quentin, March, 1918, published by Leonard and Virginia Woolf at the Hogarth Press. *English Pottery,* with Bernard Rackham.

1925   "Psychoanalysis and the Critic," *Criterion,* a pioneering essay in the application of Freudian psychology to literary criticism.

1928   *Reason and Romanticism,* his first major work in literary criticism; *English Prose Style; Phases of English Poetry.*

1929   *The Sense of Glory,* a collection of essays on writers; *Staffordshire Pottery Figures.*

1930   *Wordsworth,* the Clark Foundation Lectures, Trinity College, Cambridge.

1931   Watson Gordon Professor of Fine Arts, University of Edinburgh, 1931–1933; *The Meaning of Art* (published in the United States as *The Anatomy of Art*), based on lectures delivered on the B.B.C.

1932   *Form in Modern Poetry.*

1933   Editor, *The Burlington Magazine,* 1933–1939. *The Innocent Eye,* an autobiographical study, which was enlarged and reissued in 1947; *Art Now,* a study of contemporary art; *The End of a War,* poems.

1934   *Art and Industry.*

1935  Sydney Jones Lecturer in Art, University of Liverpool, 1935–1936. *Poems 1914–1934; The Green Child,* a fantasy; *In Defense of Shelly.*

1936  *Art and Society.*

1938  *Poetry and Anarchism; Collected Essays.*

1939  *The Knapsack.*

1940–  Leon Fellow, University of London.
1942

1943  *The Politics of the Unpolitical; Education Through Art,* based on the Leon Fellowship.

1944  *A World Within a War,* poems.

1945  *A Coat of Many Colours,* collected essays in art criticism and literary criticism.

1946  *Collected Poems.*

1947  *The Grass Roots of Art.*

1949  *Education for Peace.*

1952  *The Philosophy of Modern Art.*

1953  Created knight. Named Charles Eliot Norton Professor of Poetry, Harvard University, 1953–1954. *The True Voice of Feeling,* a study of form in modern poetry.

1954  A. W. Mellon Lecturer in Fine Arts, Washington, D.C.

1955  *Icon and Idea,* a study of the role of the visual arts in the development of the mind. *Moon's Farm,* poems.

1956 *The Art of Sculpture,* the Mellon Lectures.

1957 *The Tenth Muse,* a collection of critical essays.

1959 *A Concise History of Modern Painting.*

1960 *The Form of Things Unknown,* essays on the psychological and metaphysical basis of art and poetry.

1962 *A Letter to a Young Painter,* art essays and catalogue notices.

IT is not easy to judge the art criticism of the past objectively mainly because the materials which engage the critic do not remain the same. What Ruskin and Pater comprehended by art was vastly different from that which is known to the twentieth-century critic. Herbert Read is only one generation removed from Roger Fry, but his work reflects the tremendous expansion of the range and content of art which has occurred since the 1930's. In his own time Fry was often considered to be a radical in matters of art; from Read's point of view Fry's position with respect to modern art is virtually reactionary. It is unreasonable, of course, to expect prophetic gifts of the critic; the most we can demand is insight into the work of his contemporaries and understanding of its relationship to traditional art. Although Roger Fry was well in advance of his time in the appreciation of modern art, we ought to recognize that "modern art" is itself a highly equivocal and relative term. For Fry it signified mainly the art of Cézanne and his successors, the Post-Impressionists. In retrospect, we perceive that Fry was receptive to only one aspect of Post-Impressionist art—its revivication of the classic principle of design—and was either indifferent or hostile to other tendencies—abstraction, expressionism, surrealism, symbolism—which have since appeared to be of prime importance in the development of contemporary art.

It is not likely that Herbert Read will so soon be charged with conservatism, for the most striking characteristic of his criticism is its open-mindedness, its sympathy for change, experiment, and diversity. Read's avowed pluralism has been extremely useful to him in his role as champion and expositor of modern art in virtually all its manifestations, since to a degree unprecedented in the past the art of our time is marked by its phenomenal abundance and heterogeneity. But in evading the stigma of reaction, the pluralist runs the risk of losing his discrimination and even his standards. If one takes the chief function of the critic to be judicial, Read's work itself may be severely judged. Nor does he engage in the kind of formal or technical analysis of individual works in which Roger Fry excelled. Read regards his work as belonging to the category of philosophical criticism. It is largely theoretical, being concerned with schools and movements, with types of visual expression, and ultimately with the nature of art considered in its social and psychological relationships. It stands apart from the dominant critical mode of our time, which in literary criticism has elected to view the individual work of art as a self-contained and self-explanatory entity and to expunge "extrinsic" information from the critical act. Read would be unwilling to exclude as irrelevant any approach that illuminates either works of art or the process by which they came into being. While his own general approach may be described as genetic, seeking to explain works of art by the circumstances of their origin, one hesitates to label it. Almost from the beginning, he has employed the dialectical method, entertaining and reconciling widely opposed points of view. One of his favorite terms is "synthesis."

Read's theory of art represents the assimilation of disparate points of view drawn from a multitude of sources. Of the

critics discussed here he alone is familiar with the work of
continental writers on art. Both Bell and Fry were acutely
aware of British insularity with respect to art, and both of
them surmounted it in their attachment to French art and
culture. But their Francophilia blinded them to Northern
art as a whole and specifically to modern German scholarship, a knowledge of which is indispensable to a critic who
aspires to a comprehensive view of art. I do not wish to imply that Read adopts a partisan attitude toward the Northern as against the Mediterranean tradition. It is typical of
his method that instead of attempting to establish the priority
of one or the other, he should formulate a view broad enough
to contain both. The title of Read's first major critical work,
*Reason and Romanticism,* is symptomatic of the dialectical
approach. While confined entirely to literature, it is the
foundation of his subsequent career as a critic of literature
and of the visual arts.

Read is no less eminent as a literary critic than as an art
critic. He is convinced, furthermore, of the fundamental
unity of the arts. But there exists in his writing no trace of
the confusion of the visual arts and literature which was the
legacy of the nineteenth-century habit of apprehending art
in terms of literary content. What had been a polemical
matter for Fry—that the visual arts be perceived in terms of
plastic values rather than of the associations aroused by these
values—is axiomatic for Read. Since Fry identified this particular kind of associationism with romantic aesthetics,
Read's neo-romanticism may appear to be paradoxical until
we perceive that what Read has attempted is a fusion of formalist and expressionist aesthetics. Read's work cogently
demonstrates the continuity of British art criticism since Ruskin. The critics previously discussed were very much aware
of the inferior position of British art since the Middle Ages,
and all of them were concerned to assert the importance of
the visual arts in the face of an indifference bred on the one

hand by puritan resistance to a predominately sensuous art and on the other by an overwhelmingly literary culture. Ruskin's effort was directed to establishing painting and sculpture as modes of imagination and expression on a plane equal to literature. Partly because of his own intellectual background and temperament, partly owing to the literary flavor of the contemporary painting with which he was most familiar, Ruskin tended to blur the distinction between art and literature, and indeed between art and morality. Pater, Bell, and Fry represent in various ways the reaction against Ruskin. The emphasis of their work is analytical—to isolate, first of all, the elements which differentiate the visual arts from literature, and ultimately to separate art and morality by establishing the aesthetic integrity of those arts. The product of this separatism was a conception of pictorial form which was vindicated by modern art and which now appears to be indispensable to criticism. At the risk of considerable oversimplification, we may describe Read's achievement as the synthesis of Ruskin's romantic expressionism and Fry's formalism. Before the apparent contradictions between the two doctrines could be resolved, however, certain modifications of each had to be made. The expressionist thesis was enormously altered by means of insights into the nature of the mind provided by psychoanalysis. The conception of form, which in the case of the formalist critics had been derived from the Renaissance, or, more specifically, from the Florentine version of the classical tradition, had to be revised and expanded in order to include a wide variety of styles. Read's aim is to define the plastic or purely formal elements as symbolic or expressive, to maintain the notion of the formal integrity without at the same time insisting an absolute aesthetic autonomy.

There are indications that Fry himself at the end of his career was preparing to abandon an uncompromising formalist position. His recognition of the unconscious as the source of aesthetic emotion was a tacit though limited step in the direction of an expressionist aesthetics. More important was his introduction of sensibility and vitality as essential criteria in the judgment of art. Although Fry was not clear as to the relationship of sensibility and vitality to the classical conception of form, it seems reasonable to speculate that, in theory at least, his views were tending toward those of Read. What separates them are differences in age and temperament and background rather than aesthetic theory. In his essay on Roger Fry, Read connects Fry's chief defect as a critic—his inability to appreciate contemporary work—with his social background and education:

Faced with the machine, mass-production and universal education, he could only retreat into the private world of his own sensibility. He did, more and more as time went on, attempt to find a universal philosophic justification for this private world, and he had at his command an ingenious mind and a patient experience of his subject. But all this effort did not bring him into any very vital or sympathetic relationship to his own age.[1]

Despite Fry's apparatus of formal analysis, which bears little resemblance to the vague emotional appreciation normally associated with impressionistic criticism, Read classifies him as an impressionist. It must be admitted that there is some justification for this, since Fry was inclined to identify form in art with his own preference for forms which are susceptible of intellectual analysis and to deny formal quality to works which resisted this sort of explication. It is precisely Fry's intellectualist bias, his conviction that art is the product of the reflective and fully conscious life rather than of the instinctive life, that alienates Read. As Read points out, this conviction was not shared by the contemporary painters— Matisse and Picasso—most admired by Fry. Fry interpreted modern art as a classical revival, a return to universal formal principles. He was unsympathetic, as we have seen, to the

expressionist phase of Van Gogh and the surrealist qualities
of Picasso, as well as to nineteenth-century romantic expressionism and to German painting in general. Furthermore,
considering his lack of interest in abstract art, one perceives
the justice of Read's charge that Fry's deepest instinct was
not adventurous.

A similar accusation cannot be made of Read; his prestige
as a critic rests on his defense of modern revolutionary art,
particularly those manifestations of it which represent the
most violent break with tradition, including Tachisme and
Action Painting, which have so far proved to be intractable
not only to analysis but to critical apprehension. Read has
welcomed each new departure in art as an extension of human experience and consciousness. But we must not imagine
that his receptivity is the product of an indiscriminate eclecticism. It is based on his theory of art rather than on his preferences, which like Fry's are classical; by temperament he
is inclined to the serene, impersonal art of Piero della Francesca or Seurat. His theory, however, may be termed romantic
in that it is committed to the principle of the virtually absolute freedom of the artist's imagination: "The truth is that
art has no limits. Art is everything that can be imagined and
expressed." [2]

This for Read constitutes the central tradition of art, and
the very diversity of modern art attests to the rediscovery of
the tradition. Although he is strongly drawn to the art of
the romantic movement in painting and poetry, Read's neo-
romantic doctrine does not involve any sort of historical revival. The romantic principle is universal. Unlike the formalists, Read does not admit of any fundamental opposition
between classic and romantic art. Ruling out academic art,
which is simply bad art, he regards classic art as a category
contained within the larger whole. He is much indebted to
Nietzsche's distinction between Apollonian and Dionysian
art:

[William Blake's] art is an attempt to combine the greatest intensity of subjective thought and feeling with the greatest clarity of objective representation. And that is precisely the character of all great art—of classical art in Nietzsche's right conception of it, of Christian art in its Byzantine and early Gothic manifestations, and of the isolated art of an individual like Blake.[3]

In the tension of emotion and intellect in classical art—one of several dualistic formulations which pervade Read's work —there is no question of an equilibrium of equal and opposed forces. As far as art is concerned, the nonrational, whether we designate it as intuition, emotion, or imagination, always has priority for Read. It is possible therefore for art to dispense with reason, but a purely rational art is a contradiction in terms.

The real adversary of the romantic principle is not classical art itself, but the neo-classic doctrine:

It was inevitable that the eighteenth century, with the gradual triumph of the Cartesian philosophy and the consequent degradation of instinct and imagination, should outweigh the balance on the side of reason. And precisely that eventuality is fatal to the existence of art. Art may flourish in a rank and barbaric manner from an excess of animal vitality, but it withers and dies in the arid excesses of reason.[4]

The *locus classicus* of the rationalist theory of art is Sir Joshua Reynolds' *Discourses,* and specifically the doctrine of the grand manner, which represents for Read a degradation of classical principles. According to Reynolds,

The whole beauty and grandeur of art consists . . . in being able to get above all singular forms, local customs, particularities, and details of every kind. All objects [in] Nature, upon close examination will be found to have their blemishes and defects. . . . The Painter who aims at the greatest style . . . corrects Nature by herself, her imperfect state by her more perfect. [The painter's] eye being enabled to distinguish the accidental deficiencies, excrescences, and deformations of things, *he makes*

*out an abstract idea* of their forms more perfect than any one
original. . . . This idea of the perfect state of Nature, which the
artist calls Ideal beauty, is the great leading principle by which
works of genius are conducted.[5]

It is significant that Read dates the beginnings of modern
art from the rejection of Reynolds' doctrine by romantic artists and theorists of art. Two ideas, distinct though intimately related, are fundamental in romantic aesthetics from
the late eighteenth century to the present. The first may be
called the genetic idea, which posits an inevitable link between the work of art and the personality of the artist. The
second may be designated as primitivism, the conviction
voiced by Giambattista Vico early in the eighteenth century
that poetry represents an early stage in human development
and can be produced in modern times only by those who
are able to suspend the operations of the rational intellect by
reverting to the more primitive mental state. The ramifica-
tions of romantic aesthetics are enormously complex. There
may be no unanimity in the various romantic doctrines of
intuition and imagination nor in defining the process of artistic creation, but there is essential agreement concerning
the nonrational origins of art. According to Read, modern
art stems, if not from romantic theory itself, from the attitude
toward art engendered by the theory:

The whole of the modern tradition in art is a direct result of
such an approach to art: art is no longer conceived as a rational
ideal, a painful striving towards an intellectual perfection; but
art conceived as a stage in the ideal history of mankind, as a pre-
logical mode of expression, as something necessary and inevitable
and organic . . . the expression of imaginative heroism in the
life of the artist in any age.[6]

In his early criticism, under the influence of T. E. Hulme
perhaps, Read was inclined to make a distinction between
literature and the visual arts based on the claim that poetry,

being primarily spontaneous and intuitive in origin, was essentially a romantic art, but that the visual arts, involving a highly conscious process of composition and design, were lacking in the quality of immediacy. In his first major work devoted to the visual arts, *The Meaning of Art* (1931), he was of the opinion that in spite of certain romantic conceptions the main tendency of modern art had been toward a reintegration of the intellect. Read was thinking primarily of Cubism and geometrically abstract art. But a more thorough absorption in modern art led Read to abandon the distinction; in his later work even the more ostensibly intellectual manifestations of modern art are conceived as falling within the general hypothesis concerning the intuitive nature of artistic creation.

Read's career as a writer on art coincides not only with the explosive development of modern art itself but also with an enormous expansion of knowledge concerning the art of the past which has had a shattering effect on an aesthetics confined chiefly to European painting since the early Renaissance. Modern art and its rationale reflect that knowledge and also a parallel expansion of knowledge provided by psychology, anthropology, and the physical and biological sciences. Nineteenth-century romantic critical theory was predicated upon somewhat analogous circumstances—awareness of the diversity of national cultures, the renewal of interest in early national art, and a concomitant predilection for the primitive and childlike. The permanent contributions of romantic theory, however, were the notion of the primacy of emotion over intellect in art and the concept of imagination as the means whereby the subjective experience of the artist is transmuted into artistic expression. Ruskin's art criticism assumes a significance for Herbert Read which is in sharp contrast with the attitude of the nineteenth-century aesthetes and the twentieth-century formalists toward his work. Read holds Ruskin's application of the theory of the imagination to

the visual arts to be absolutely on a par with Coleridge's contribution to literary theory. Ruskin's statements on the emotive, expressive power of painting are as eloquent as one can
find in the whole literature of art criticism, but in practice
his expressionist views are remarkably ambiguous, owing
chiefly to his almost exclusive concern with what Read calls
the realistic, but what might better be called the representational, aspects of art. As we have seen, the main effort of art
criticism after Ruskin was devoted to disentangling the specifically aesthetic values in painting from the representational
or imitative values. In the process of arriving at the conclusion that the aesthetic effect was exclusively the product of
purely pictorial (that is, plastic) form to which representation was almost totally irrelevant, the formalist critics decided that the peculiarly aesthetic property of form derived
from the uniqueness of the emotion it evoked. Hence they
denied the visual arts an expressive function in any ordinarily accepted sense. Partly because his aesthetics is not
nearly so bound up with European painting, Read goes much
farther than the formalists with respect to representational
art:

Sculpture is the creation of solid forms which give aesthetic
pleasure. There is an infinite variety of such forms, and they
arise and are proliferated by laws which are formal and not
representational. . . . Nothing in the history of art is so fatal as
the representational fallacy; nowhere, in the history of art, is that
fatality so inevitable as in the evaluation of sculpture. Repeatedly
the art dies of this disease.[7]

Read, then affirms the formalist postulate concerning the
primacy of form without at the same time accepting the
idea of its autotelic existence. Read is therefore able to arrive at the insight of which Ruskin was incapable—that form
itself is the vehicle of expression and imagination, and hence
that form is essentially symbolic.

The reconciliation of form and expression is the actual conclusion toward which Read's aesthetic speculation tended for
many years; it was reached, not by a direct route, but by
means of the dialectical process which is so characteristic of
Read's thought. One of the important steps was his entirely
original perception that the distinguishing feature of romantic art is its form, first thoroughly articulated in *The
True Voice of Feeling* (1953), a volume devoted to modern
poetry. But he is also aware of the relevance of form to
painting:

What was revolutionary [in romanticism] was the recognition of
sensibility itself as the raw material of literature and painting.
. . . What is essential to romanticism is not its content, but its
form. . . . To identify form with substance—that is precisely the
romantic revolution. The essential notion is that literature . . .
is a *formative activity*. Form emerges spontaneously from the
poet's intuitive apprehension of the thought . . . or from [the
painter's] plastic realization of the image present to his mind.[8]

There are several instances in which Read's preoccupation
with form may lend him the appearance of an aestheticism
which is at variance with his fundamental view of art as
integrally related to the springs of human life. The following
statement, as a matter of fact, is written in support of Pater's
celebrated passage on music as the model of the arts in "The
School of Giorgione"—one of the landmarks of formalist
criticism:

At the end of many centuries of critical consideration, and in
virtue of a vast amount of accumulated wisdom, there seems no
avoiding the conclusion, that if we are to keep our aesthetic
judgments, whether in poetry, painting, or music, clear of all irrelevant facts, then those judgments must be based on the opera-
tive sensibilities, and on those sensibilities alone. No criticism that
is not a criticism of form in its relation to subject-matter has
ever advanced any of the arts a single step. The virtue of any

art wholly inheres in its appeal to the senses and to the "non-discursive" or "imaginative" reason, and all other criteria, whether moral or sociological, are *aesthetically* irrelevant. It is a criticism of wider scope and a different kind that attempts to relate aesthetic values to their social environment—to explain the distortions which these values suffer in the historical circumstances of a particular period, and in the estimation of all succeeding periods. It is sometimes necessary, however, to maintain the autonomy of art, as of philosophy, however abstract and theoretical such an attitude may seem.[9]

There is nothing here to which Roger Fry could not have wholeheartedly subscribed; yet even if Read was much closer to Fry's position at this time (1934) than he was later, there are important divergences, particularly in the conception of form itself. For instance, Read does not imply by "criticism of form" the kind of formal analysis by which Fry is best known. We recall that Fry's analysis was mainly directed at those aspects of sensibility which could be reduced to rational terms, such as the logic, coherence, and harmony of plastic and spatial elements in painting. It is obvious that Fry's interest lay in what we might call "constructed" forms, those which give evidence of deliberate and fully conscious control. Read is willing to grant the relevance of rational formal analysis to such constructions, but for him the really significant aspect of forms in art is their spontaneous, largely unconscious origin. The conscious shaping of intuited forms is merely the superstructure, not the basis of art:

Form, though it can be analysed into intellectual terms like measure, balance, rhythm and harmony, is really intuitive in origin; it is not in the actual practice of artists an intellectual product. It is rather emotion directed and defined . . . when we describe art as "the will to form," we are not imagining an exclusively intellectual activity, but rather an exclusively instinctive one. . . . Frankly, I do not know how we are to judge form except by the same instinct that creates it.[10]

From the point of view of contemporary literary criticism, which is predominantly analytical and committed to an ideal conception of the work of art as an autonomous object, self-contained and self-explanatory insofar as its aesthetic properties are concerned, Read's attitude might be construed as an abrogation of criticism. He has himself acknowledged the divergence of his work from normal practice:

But what, if not philosophic, is this activity I have indulged in . . . for the best part of a lifetime? It is not critical, for I have never pretended to assess the value of particular works of art, or to arrange artists in an hierarchy of worth. It is not historical, for although I am conscious of connections, and eager to trace the re-emergence of traditions, I am not systematic enough to give the complete picture of a period, nor confident enough to define a school or classify a generation. The method I adopt may be called philosophic because it is the affirmation of a value-judgment. To be precise, I believe that among the agents or instruments of human evaluation, art is extremely important. I believe that the aesthetic faculty has been the means of man first acquiring, and then refining, consciousness. Form, the progressive organization of elements otherwise chaotic, is given in perception . . . The realization of formal values is the aesthetic activity.[11]

As we see, Read's theory of visual art preserves the formalists' awareness of the primacy of form without sacrificing Ruskin's conviction that art is profoundly and intimately connected with human concerns. But Read's ultimate insight into the significance of visual form was made possible by his recognition of the multiplicity of forms. It was the very fact of their diversity which provided the clue to the conception of the visual arts as the primary agency in the shaping of the mind.

Read's investigations of the phenomenon of form follows two main avenues—psychological and historical—but he has not hesitated to draw upon all and sundry sources of knowledge in order to understand and to explain art. His chief debt, however, is to the general theory of psychoanalysis and particularly to the work of Jung. The evidence provided by psychoanalysis of a whole segment of psychic activity, hitherto unknown or only vaguely sensed, not only corroborated the central tenet of romantic criticism—that the essential elements in art are intuitive and irrational—but also suggested new solutions of problems in aesthetics which had been posed by the abandonment of the classical doctrine of beauty as the standard for judging and interpreting art. Read's art theory is not tied to any specific sectarian view of the structure of personality, but rather to the general hypothesis concerning the existence of a level of mental activity lying below that of consciousness, ordinarily hidden from us and leading a life of its own. As Read sees it, the idea of the unconscious provided a new key to the concept of the mind implicit in the romantic theory of imagination. It destroyed the age-old belief that art is mimesis and proved the interiority of artistic creation. Because the hypothesis is even more momentous for the practicing artist than for the critic, Read calls it "the sustaining myth": "These hidden springs now have a name: the unconscious . . . vitalizing all the arts (even where most abstract) is the sustaining myth of the unconscious. The mirror has been shattered, and behind it we have found the cave of Dionysus, a cave of inexhaustible wonder." [12]

Although the ultimate test of the validity of the neo-romantic aesthetics is one of universality, there can be little doubt concerning its appositeness to contemporary art, which is overwhelmingly dedicated to interior vision, ranging from radically idiosyncratic versions of the external world to its complete abandonment. Quite apart from movements which came into being through a deliberate and self-conscious use of psychoanalysis, notably Surrealism, modern art as a whole is illuminated by the psychoanalytic approach. Read's great success as a proponent of modern art undoubtedly owes much

to his early recognition of this fact. His first essays in psychoanalytic criticism were literary, and these were mainly
concerned with subject matter rather than with form. It
was not until he applied this knowledge to the visual arts
that Read discovered the relevance of the unconscious to the
formal or strictly aesthetic elements in art. It will be recalled
that Clive Bell's doctrine of significant form had an instan-
taneous success and remained virtually indispensable in aesthetic discourse in spite of the fact that Bell himself was at
a loss to account for the significance of form. The hypothesis
of the origin of form in the unconscious goes far to clarify
the hitherto inexplicable significance of the abstract, perceptual configurations which Bell took to be the essence of
art. The neo-romantic aesthetics resolves the paradox inherent in the formalist position, but at the expense of an autotelic, dehumanized conception of form.

A tendency inherent in all romantic theories of art, to
which Read's is no exception, is to reduce aesthetic experience
to private, subjective experience. Read's belief in the subjectivity of aesthetic experience—a constant factor in all his
criticism—is confirmed by the formal qualities of modern
art:

The theorist of modern art, in defence of Matisse, must claim
that no definition of painting which does not include in some way
the concept of FORM can survive application for long. . . . The
thing formed—and this is the clue to the whole of the modern
development of art—can be subjective as well as objective—can
be the emergent sensibility of the artist himself.[13]

The postulate of form as emergent sensibility, as the direct,
unmediated embodiment of subjective emotion, annihilates
the possibility not only of rational analysis but indeed of an
objective criterion of form, such as was implied in the neo-
classic doctrine of beauty as an ideal version of nature or of
Roger Fry's concept of plastic order which Read takes to be

a variant of idealism. The inadequacy of Fry's unitary conception of form is pointed up by its almost total irrelevance to the work of an artist like Paul Klee, which has had extraordinary importance in the development of modern art. Read takes direct issue with Fry, however, not on the question of modern art but on that of Turner:

The truth is that for many years now the issue of Turner's art has been avoided by art critics, English and American. "Avoided" is perhaps not the right word, since some of these critics, such as Roger Fry, have expressed themselves in no uncertain terms. It is the real issue that has been avoided, and this is the clash I have already spoken of, between the Northern and Mediterranean traditions, between Expressionism and Idealism. I do not think that any of the exponents of Expressionism least of all Ruskin, have wished to deny the values represented by the classical ideal. But they do insist that it is not the only way of representing the world we experience. . . . We experience the world through the subtle medium of a temperament, and if we faithfully represent that experience, we produce something unique, or at any rate, something typical of our temperament. In the end, all differences of style reduce to differences of temperament. If we now assume that the artist is at liberty to express his temperament in painting, then there ought to be as many types of painting as there are types of persons, and this is indeed what we find.[14]

The polarity of Northern and Mediterranean styles which Read derived from Heinrich Wölfflin is one of a series of stylistic classifications that have reinforced Read's pluralistic approach to art. Wölfflin's distinction between Northern and Mediterranean is almost exclusively based on the formal properties of European art from the Middle Ages through the Baroque. The difference in style is attributed to profound psychological differences in the respective peoples. The prime quality of Mediterranean or Classical form is clarity of contour, sharp definition, and the marked articulation of the subject from its surroundings. The emphasis is entirely on visibility and rationality. The characteristic of Northern or Gothic, on the other hand, is the interlocking or interlacing of figures, the coalescence of the object and its background. According to Wölfflin, Northern style strives to represent or embody a transcendental reality, whereas Classical is concerned with the visible. Another, and for Herbert Read an even more important classification of forms, is that of Wilhelm Worringer, whose aesthetics has had a direct influence on the theory and practice of twentieth-century artists. Worringer's distinction between abstraction and empathy, between geometrical and organic forms, has a much wider range of reference than Wölfflin's, extending over the whole range of art. His hypothesis applies, for instance, to the radical difference in the styles of Paleolithic and Neolithic art. Worringer's classification also assumes that style is both psychological and social in origin, deriving from the fundamental attitude of a society toward the visible universe. Abstract, geometrical forms are associated with societies oppressed by nature, and hence preoccupied with nonmaterial (that is, spiritual) reality; organic forms with societies which are aware of a sense of unity with nature and find spiritual satisfaction in the visible world.

Both these systems of classification are the products of art historians and contain marked metaphysical overtones. Read has also turned to experimental psychology in his search for a hypothesis to account for the diversity of forms in the visual arts. He has been struck by Viktor Löwenfeld's *Nature of Creative Activity* which discloses the existence of a specifically haptic sensibility as distinguished from the visual sensibility. The distinction here is physiological or somatic rather than philosophical: haptic images are produced by persons who apprehend form primarily in terms of muscular and nervous tensions. Read's treatise on the role of education in art adopts as a central assumption the fallacy of a uniform style or tradition and art. His own fourfold classification is a synthesis of previous distinctions. According to Read the types of aesthetic perception correspond respectively to four kinds of mental activity—thinking, feeling, sensation, intuition: (1) realism or naturalism, (2) idealism, romanticism, super-realism, fantastic or imaginative art—all these transform images of visual origin into an independent reality, (3) expressionism—the discovery of plastic equivalents for immediate sensations, (4) abstract, constructive art—a style which attempts to avoid all personal elements, employing the purely formal relationships of space, mass, and color.

Although there are historical grounds for Read's pluralism, it is fairly evident that its strongest justification is the overwhelming diversity of modern art, which poses insuperable problems for traditional analytic and judicial criticism. Read's receptivity to the widest possible variety of artistic expression has kept him aloof from the battle of schools and styles. Although he firmly believes that the formal attributes of art, being intuitive or unconscious in origin, must be intuitively grasped by the spectator and therefore evade rational apprehension, he does not necessarily abandon the possibility of an objective judgment. He has steadily explored the means for discovering a mode of aesthetic judgment which transcends a purely subjective response. At one period he accepted the perceptual theory of Gestalt psychology as the best explanation of the nature of form in the visual arts. The doctrine of "psychophysical isomorphism" attributes the aesthetic acceptability of forms to their conformity with the demands of perception, which is predisposed toward images providing physical comfort and clarity. At one point, Read interprets Cézanne's formal revolution as the achievement of "good Gestalt." While the theory is undoubtedly illuminating with respect to predominantly visual forms, it is not so useful in connection with expressionist art.

In the long run, Read's search for values depends on the

authority of nature rather than on any specific scientific doctrine:

Relativism does not necessarily imply an absence of judgment. It can, of course, be maintained that all values, whether moral or aesthetic, are as relative as the experiences we call art, and in a sense this is true. . . . The more consciously moral or political values are imposed on art, the more art suffers. Art is spontaneous, the unpremeditated act of an individual, but always innocent. Where, then, does it find its scale of values? On what basis can we judge all the heterogeneous manifestations of art, if not by social or ethical standards? . . . *In nature.* There, absolute and universal, is a touchstone for all human artifacts—not in any vague pantheistic spirit, but the measurements and physical behavior of matter in any process of growth or transformation.[15]

The appeal to nature is in accord with Read's profession of romanticism. It is entirely consistent with his belief in the spontaneous mode of artistic creation and with his rejection of artistic form as something externally imposed upon the work whether by rules or tradition or social authority. But Read's appeal to nature is not connected, as Ruskin's was, with the imitation of nature. The parallel between the forms of visual art and those of nature consists not in external appearances but in structural principles biologically determined. The distinction is fully discussed in Read's essay on Ben Nicholson:

The mechanical manipulation of geometrical elements has nothing in common with the constructive vision displayed in the work of an artist like Ben Nicholson, and only the ambiguity inherent in the word "abstract" could have given rise to such an impression. If the word is quite rightly used to indicate an art that renounced any intention of reproducing the *natural appearances* of *phenomena,* it does not necessarily imply a loss of all contact with reality. The basic confusion is between two very different things: reality and realism. Art, the critics of constructivism say, cannot safely depart from nature. But what do they mean by nature? Actually a philosophical question is involved. Nature is either an aggregate of facts—the sum of all organic things; or it is the principle of life which animates these things. If we think of nature in the first, and what we may call the objective sense, and consider the function of art in relation to such a conception of nature, then we can conceive of art only as reproducing in some way the specific facts. That is, indeed, the kind of relation between art and nature which most people seem to want, but they should realize that what they thus get is not the reality, but merely the appearances of nature. If, on the other hand, we take the subjective conception of nature, and then ask the artist to express this conception in the materials of his craft, he will not imitate the specific appearances of nature, but taking it in the sense he has of the underlying spirit, he will try to create works which embody this spirit in their form and colour. These works will have a kind of cousinship with the phenomenon of nature, but being moulded not by the sun and soil and all the elements which determine the specific forms of natural organisms, but rather by the senses of the artist reacting to plastic material, they will have an original appearance reflecting nothing but the reality experienced by the individual.[16]

The criterion of naturalism is employed here as the basis for a value judgment that discriminates between academic abstraction which merely manipulates its materials in a mechanical fashion and abstraction which reveals genuine constructive vision. It may seem strange that Read perceives vitality to be the principle underlying the severe geometrical abstractions of Ben Nicholson, since the term is usually associated with organic forms. Read himself, under the influence of Worringer's dualistic classification, makes a distinction between vitality and beauty: "The term 'aesthetic' covers two very different psychological processes—one tending to an emphasis on *vitality,* the other discovering the still centre, the balance and harmony of beauty. . . . In general the artist has had to choose between the path of vitality and the path of beauty." [17] Since Read's allegiance to the predominantly organic forms of Henry Moore is equal to his admiration for the geometrical, abstract art of Ben Nicholson and Naum Gabo, he is inclined to minimize the distinction, without actually resolving it:

All psychological types, all phenomenal variations whatsoever, are equally "natural," and the realities of art, as they must be expressed in any criticism which pretends to be more than the expression of personal prejudices, must relate to the normal, the fundamental . . . rather than to the "accidentality" or "incidentality" of the formulation of such principles. The cabbage is just as natural as the crystal, and the natural laws underlying these phenomena are essentially identical. . . . To prefer the organic to the constructive is merely to express a prejudice. . . . However much we may insist that the constructive work is no less justified in nature than the organic work, there will always be a tendency to associate the organic with the vital and therefore with the human.[18]

It should be fairly evident that Read's discussion of art is mainly conducted on the aesthetic level, that he is not on the whole distracted by matters extrinsic to the work of art. Yet his general outlook is far removed from that of the formalists who contend that the distinctive feature of aesthetic experience is its isolation from all nonaesthetic experience. Read is as much concerned as Clive Bell and Roger Fry to preserve the autonomy of aesthetic judgment from ethical and practical criteria, and yet from the very beginning he has doubted the hypothesis of the uniqueness and autonomy of aesthetic experience and has explored its relationship to "life." The formalists, it should be noted, were concerned primarily with representational art, and their aim was to disengage plastic form from the irrelevant or nonessential elements with which it was associated, particularly the literary content of paintings. Since such abstract formal properties as line, mass, and color are themselves very remote from literary content, the formalists assumed that they were therefore totally unrelated to ordinary, that is, nonaesthetic, human experience. Read, however, works within a frame of reference of abstract and nonobjective art in which pictorial form appears in a relatively pure state, disassociated not only from literary content but often from representation. The purity of form no longer being at stake, he was free to concentrate on the problems of how visual forms, however abstract and remote from ordinary human experience they appear, are connected with that experience. The conclusion he arrived at eventually was that visual forms are integrally involved in the development of consciousness, that aesthetic experience is actually a mode of knowledge, aesthetic perception having actually preceded conceptual knowledge in human development, thus constituting the basis of thought.

Actually both Bell and Fry had very tentatively proposed the possibility of the cognitive function of aesthetic experience, suggesting that plastic forms revealed a certain order of reality, but they were unwilling to pursue the metaphysical implications of that suggestion. But this awareness did not alter their fundamental conviction that aesthetic experience has little or no bearing on man's life in society. Read's speculations, on the other hand, lead to a reaffirmation, not of course of Ruskin's moralistic judgments of individual works, but of his underlying view of the social and moral role of art. Once again it is modern art which provides insight into the cognitive nature of aesthetic experience; Read does not hesitate to follow Ruskin in asserting truth to be the aim of art:

For good or ill we now demand from the artist an expression of *truth;* and in judging the success of the artist in this task our criterion is the subjective criterion of vitality rather than the objective criterion of harmony. We say of a work of art that it moves us, that it appeals to us, that it fascinates us, that it excites us—all expressions that indicate a psychological and not an intel-

lectual reaction. We have revalued the art of the past in the same
subjective way and have nothing but contempt for the aesthetic
judgments of the eighteenth and nineteenth centuries. In this
revaluation of aesthetic values from beauty to truth, from idealism to realism, from serenity to vitality—the whole of the modern
movement of art, beginning with Impressionism, is involved as
a practical activity and the whole of the modern criticism of art
is involved as a philosophical activity. . . . Our real aim is to
treat the infinitely complex range and subtle intricacy of human
sensibility as an instrument for the apprehension of reality—of
reality in its widest sense. . . . Our objective is not pleasure or it
is pleasure only incidentally. We have discovered that art has a
biological function, that the artist, like the photosynthetic cells
that absorb creative energy from cosmic rays, is the sensitive
organ of an evolving consciousness—of man's progressive apprehension and understanding of his universe.[19]

   This statement makes two sweeping assertions. The first
of these is a total rejection of the hedonistic function of art
which was explicitly declared by the late nineteenth-century
aesthetes and implicit in the twentieth-century formalist view
of art as an end in itself. The second, which claims art as an
instrument of knowledge, is not irrelevant to aesthetics, but
the view of the mind which it promulgates properly belongs to the province of philosophy or psychology. The testimony of contemporary artists on this score is not uniform.
Whereas some abstract artists have not claimed for their
work any aim beyond that of the creation of pure forms as
ends in themselves, others, particularly those who are committed to nonobjective art, have assigned a cognitive function
to their work. From Kandinsky onward abstract artists have
subscribed to the view that plastic forms actually embody an
insight into spiritual reality. Such a view is common to both
expressionists and constructivists, by the proponents of organic and those of geometrical forms. Read himself is not
inclined to discount the artist's credo:

Ben Nicholson who, like all the great artists of the past, is something of a mystic, believes that there is a reality underlying appearances, and that it is his business, by giving material form to his intuition of it, to express the essential nature of this reality. He does not draw that intuition of reality out of a vacuum, but out of a mind attuned to the specific awareness of the proportions and harmonies inherent in all natural phenomena in the universe itself.[20]

The testimony of the artist does not, of course, guarantee the validity of the hypothesis concerning the cognitive function of aesthetic experience, but it does illuminate the aims of modern art. It is difficult, if not impossible, to describe or to explain the enterprise of modern art in its totality—its almost desperate experimentation, its apocalyptic visions, its rupture with the "normal," its pursuit of the occult—by means of formalist theory. As Malraux has observed, modern art in its seriousness and in its rejection of material appearances is not only conditioned by the disintegration of religious belief in our time, but has itself become a religious undertaking, a heroic effort to penetrate to the numinous. Both Fry and Bell had hinted at the correspondence of significant form and spiritual reality, but they generally mean by spiritual that which transcends the practical activity rather than the transcendence of material reality. Read's objection to the formalist method is directed against its materialist bias:

Certain of the earlier phases of modern art—the paintings of Cézanne, those of the Cubists—lent themselves all too easily to the formalistic method. But this method becomes meaningless when applied to a picture like Picasso's "Guernica," to a painting by Klee or Max Ernst, to Kokoschka's "Windbrant" or Chagall's "Russian Village"; or generally to the art of the last thirty years [1922-1952]. Such artists are using other means, other conventions, to secure the desired effect, and a new type of art must call into existence a new type of art criticism. . . . Modern art—Picasso,

Braque, Klee, Henry Moore—is far more akin to Byzantine art
than to the art of any intervening period. . . . Its philosophical
basis—and for a modern man his philosophy is often his religion
—is equally a denial of the validity of the real, and art is consequently an attempt to express a mystery, which we have not confidence enough to call the Truth. . . . All that is essentially
modern in contemporary art is in some sense super realistic. . . .
The modern critic can never for a moment ignore the purely
plastic values by means of which aesthetic pleasure is communicated; but these plastic values are now used once more in the
service of what might be called metaphysical values, and the
critic's function is again to render in adequate words the significance of the symbols created by the artist.[21]

Read adopts the primary postulate of formalist criticism
concerning the identification of the aesthetic constitution of
the work of art with its formal elements, but the formalists'
contention that formal values are devoid of expressive or symbolic function is quite foreign to Read's essentially romantic
outlook. In the earlier stages of his aesthetics, artistic expression was largely identified with emotions which have their
origin in the unconscious; consequently, he envisaged plastic
forms as the concrete embodiment of those emotions and
enunciated a doctrine of the unity of form and feeling. The
preoccupation with feeling as the basis of art is less pronounced in his later work. A growing conviction of the cognitive function of the visual arts, which was strengthened by
his communications with contemporary artists themselves
and by the effect of their work, brought about certain modifications of his ideas of form. Although he was concerned
solely with meanings or content that could be conveyed by
plastic means, he was in doubt whether form and symbol
could actually be submitted to a single judgment or apprehended as a unified phenomenon. He was led to make a clear-
cut distinction between the aesthetic and cognitive functions
of art and indeed between two distinct kinds of art, that

which is primarily imagistic and that which is primarily
symbolic:

It has been claimed that the capacity for realizing and retaining
the image in a state of perceptive vividness is the quality that distinguishes the artist—the imagist. . . . At the other extreme of
artistic practice the artist abandons himself freely to a symbolical
activity. . . . An artist of the symbolist type is creating a combination of forms and colours . . . which will convey a meaning,
and in art this meaning always has an aesthetic or emotional
tinge. Art of this kind may therefore be defined as "the symbolic
transfer of emotion" . . .[22] The main distinction between these
two types of art appears to be in the orientation of one towards
an external, sensational reality, of the other towards an inner,
subjective emotion. The latter, however, acquires aesthetic qualities only by virtue of conforming to the laws of the visible: as
soon as we attempt to translate unconscious phenomena into perceptual images, the instinctive laws of perception intervene—we
automatically project the good Gestalt, the composition that obeys
aesthetic laws.[23]

It appeared to Read that the polarity of aesthetic values and
symbolic content cannot be resolved, and that most of the
contradictions and variety of modern art could be attributed
to the antithetical nature of these elements. He can perceive
no compromise between the formalist point of view as represented by Cézanne and the symbolist approach of Gauguin,
nor does a synthesis seem to Read either possible or desirable.
    There is an analogy here to the dilemma concerning the
fusion of plastic and "psychological" values in art which was
central to Roger Fry's aesthetics. Fry, as we know, concluded that no true synthesis was possible and that the plastic
formal values alone constituted the basis of art. Read, at this
point, believed that symbolic elements were not intrinsically
aesthetic and acquired aesthetic value only by transformation
into plastic form. Read, of course, was not disturbed by the
necessity of having to maintain a pluralistic view of modern

art, but in this instance his confidence in the dialectical method seems to have been justified, for in a later phase of his work he does attempt to establish the synthesis of image and symbol or, to employ his new terminology, of "icon and idea." In the book which bears that title he describes the whole history of art as "the piecemeal recognition and patient fixation of what is significant in human experience" and defines artistic activity as "a crystallization from the amorphous realm of feeling, of forms that are significant or symbolic." [24]

It is worth noting that the formalist phrase "significant form" is echoed here, but radically altered in meaning, since, contrary to its original intention, "significant" is openly equated with "symbolic." The opposition between image and symbol, between the aesthetic and the cognitive function of art, is resolved, first of all, by expanding the concept of the aesthetic: "The specifically aesthetic act is to take possession of a revealed segment of the real; to establish its dimension and to define its form. Reality is thus what we articulate, and what we articulate is communicable only in virtue of its aesthetic form." [25] The term "symbol" has acquired a much broader denotation than it had in formalist aesthetics. In the present context, all the products of the mind are regarded as symbolic and the mind itself as a symbol-forming entity. For this idea, Read is directly indebted to Ernst Cassirer's philosophy of symbolic forms. In Read's paraphrase, each authentic function of the mind involves an original, formative power. Art, myth, religion, cognition "all live in particular image-worlds, which do not merely reflect the empirically given, but which rather produce it in accordance with an independent principle." Each of these mental activities creates its own symbolic forms, which are of equal rank: "None of these forms can be simply reduced to, or derived from, the others; each of them designates a particular approach, in which and through which it constitutes its own aspect of 'reality.'" [26] Carried out to its ultimate implications for aesthetics, Cassirer's philosophy, besides lending support to Read's intrinsic conviction of the cognitive power of art, tends to destroy the distinction between aesthetic experience and other psychic activity which had been so prominent in the formalistic aesthetics.

The subtitle of Read's *Icon and Idea* is "The Function of Art in the Development of Human Consciousness." The work is designed to demonstrate that the visual arts have had a decisive role in the evolution of the mind and that aesthetic activity precedes intellectual development in virtually all the crucial stages of that evolution. Primarily it is a contribution to the theory of the mind rather than a treatise on art; but quite irrespective of its success in that aim and of Read's competence in philosophy, it serves as a valuable summation of his speculations on art. The approach is chronological, beginning with prehistoric art. If, with Read, we reject the hypothesis that the cave paintings are a byproduct of ritualistic magic, they would appear to offer considerable evidence for Read's main contention concerning the evolution of the mind. His treatment of prehistoric art, however, has great relevance to his theory of art, in that it establishes categories which have remained constant in the subsequent development of art. The distinction between the organic animal style of the Paleolithic wall paintings and the geometrical style of Neolithic artifacts is not so crucial as it would seem according to Worringer's theory. Whereas Worringer attributed the difference between the organic and the geometrical styles to profound psychological differences, for Read the geometrical style does not constitute a renunciation of the organic image but a transformation of it brought about by a new mental capacity for abstraction, which was itself derived from the technical activities of basket weaving and the manipulation of clay. The important fact is that both styles are vitalistic in principle, geometrical art being a variant of naturalistic art. As far as the basic image in art is concerned, there is then no distinction. The important contribution of Neolithic art, for Read, is the principle of composition, involving the relationship of several images, whereas Paleolithic art was devoted to the single, "eidetic" image:

For centuries of aesthetic development the composition was to be the essence of the work of art: art was conceived as a process of composition. But the composition, with its laws of harmony and proportion, its unity and serenity, what is it but the paradigm of that intellectual ideal which the Greeks were to call *to kalon,* and which we call beauty. What in the course of the Neolithic period had been born was therefore the first consciousness of beauty. It is the second great principle in art, the first being vitality, established in the Paleolithic period.[27]

It will be noted that within the framework of the formal, that is, the aesthetic, Read has established still another duality replacing the earlier one of organic vs. geometrical forms:

The term "aesthetic" covers two very different psychological processes—one tending to an emphasis on *vitality,* the other discovering the still centre, the balance and harmony of beauty. The contemplation of beauty left the sensibility out of the stress of life. . . . In general the artist has had to choose between the path of vitality and the path of beauty.[28]

I think we can detect in this formulation the residue of Read's earlier preoccupation with the classic-romantic antithesis. It is interesting that Read revives the concept of beauty, which has generally been abandoned in contemporary aesthetics and that it has in his context a definitely classical connotation recalling eighteenth-century aesthetics, particularly Winckelmann's characterization of Greek art. Beauty, evidently, is susceptible of formal analysis, since it involves relationships which can be intellectually grasped, which actually correspond to the workings of the intellect.

Vitality, on the other hand, is inexplicable. That the symbols evolved for economic or utilitarian purposes by Paleolithic art should acquire a vitalistic aesthetic quality remains for Read a mystery. Furthermore, aesthetic response to vital images can be recorded only in terms of intensity of feeling or intuitive recognition.

The next section of *Icon and Idea* deals with the transcendental element in Christian art, the creation of symbols for the numinous. Read is less concerned with the stylistic characteristics of Gothic than with propounding the bold hypothesis that, contrary to the accepted mode of regarding Gothic art as an emanation of the medieval mind, it was actually the aesthetic realization of space in the dome and the vault that gave rise to the concept of transcendence, thereby illustrating his general thesis that the structure of thought is consequent upon the artist's discovery of symbols for the representation of reality. Not only transcendentalism, but humanism as a mental structure, is attributed to the discoveries of visual artists. Here Read reverses the chronological pattern, going back to the sculpture of Greece.

It was no doubt inevitable that sooner or later man should attempt to comprehend and represent the subjective source of all the images and symbols he creates in his attempt to construct an external reality—that he should attempt to realize and represent the Self. There were two possibilities: to become conscious of what is unique in each individual—his subjectivity; or to become conscious of what was common to all men—their humanity.[29]

The latter was, of course, the contribution of Greek art, a development and rationalization of the principle which first appeared in Neolithic art; the former does not occur until the beginning of the modern era in the Renaissance.

As we approach the present, the role of the visual arts in the shaping of the consciousness becomes increasingly difficult both to trace and to demonstrate. The Renaissance inaugurated a situation in which the processes of art proceed as the basis of tropes and images which are not directly derived from individual experience but are so many counters acquired in the cultural exchange. Schools and academies are established which teach men not to use their senses, not to cultivate their awareness of the visible world, but to accept certain canons of expression, and from these to construct theoretical devices whose subtlety appeals to reason rather than sensibility. Art becomes a game played according to conventional rules.[30]

Nevertheless, in spite of what Read regards as the greatest handicaps to art—convention and rationality—the visual arts continued to extend man's explorations of reality and hence the dimensions of the mind, notably in the Florentines' discovery of the illusion of the presence of objects in free space which Read credits to Masaccio. The architectonic aspects of Florentine painting have great relevance to the development of scientific thought in the Western world. But, Read believes, the prodigious skill required to construct an illusion of space based on the perspectival coherence of objects situated in it became an end in itself rather than a means for creating symbols for feeling or intuition, and the decadence of European art, lasting nearly four centuries, set in.

The sterility of European art was not to be overcome so long as illusionism remained the prime motive of the artist. The spell is not broken until the emergence of modern art, which Read perceives as taking two principal directions—an art of the Self, related to the humanistic aspect of Greek art but distinguished from it by its emphasis on unique, subjective experience, and a relatively impersonal, constructive art. The first has its origins in the romantic movement and its discovery of the reality of the consciousness itself—subjective reality as against the illusion of the real; it culminates in our own time in Surrealism, Expressionism in various manifestations, and finally in automatic art. The second, which seeks images of harmony rather than of vitality, may be said to originate with Cézanne. We recall that Roger Fry perceived in Cézanne's achievement the rediscovery of the classic values of plastic form, but ignored Cézanne's deliberate effort to come to grips with nature in the sense of external reality. Read's interpretation is probably more faithful to the facts:

Cézanne's agonized career as a painter is to be understood as an attempt to realize an objective world without abandoning the sensuous basis of his aesthetic experience. He always uses the verb *réaliser* in this transitive sense. . . . Art is its own reality: it is the revelation or creation of an objective world, not the representation of one. This was Cézanne's great, though perhaps incidental, discovery. He found himself giving to reality—to real things like mountains, trees, and people—a structural configuration which was not the surface appearance of these things but rather their supporting geometry, their spatial depth, their immaculate colors devoid of high lights or shadows. His pictures became what he called "constructions after nature, based on the methods, the sensations and developments suggested by the model." In Cézanne's case this process of realization was never . . . analytical; it was a struggle to achieve a pure state of consciousness before the natural object.[31]

Thus the constructivist art of Cézanne, no less than the more obviously vitalistic post-romantic art, issues from subjective emotion and intuition.

Read's historical study concludes with the further development of Cézanne's discovery in the work of artists such as Juan Gris, Mondrian, and Naum Gabo. Undoubtedly Read's effort to convert aesthetic experience entirely into a cognitive activity is too ambitious, too sweeping. Yet even if he does not succeed in establishing his contention that the visual arts constitute the foundation of philosophy, he has made it abundantly clear that sensibility has played a far more significant role in human development than is usually granted by an excessively rational and verbally oriented culture, and that in consequence art has a greater importance for society than even Ruskin was able to perceive. In the long run, Read's distinction as a critic will rest less on his aesthetics and his almost singlehanded reanimation of the romantic principle, than on his recognition of the relevance of art to the human condition. His writings on art recapture the ethical emphasis which has been missing in English art criticism since Ruskin, but unlike Ruskin, Read has always avoided the subordination of aesthetics to any a priori system, ethical or otherwise. His procedure is exactly the reverse of this; his ethical, social, and political views are essentially the outgrowth of his aesthetic experience. Read's politics—a version of philosophical anarchism—is intimately related to ideas of spontaneity and freedom which have their origin in the romantic view of art.

Read's valuation of art as the supreme means of social and moral regeneration is linked with his naturalism, his belief that the production of art is a natural—that is, biological— activity. The atrophy of the aesthetic instinct and its effect on artistic creativity is bound to have serious consequences for society:

Art, in my opinion, has remained a key to survival. However much it may have been smothered in false idealism and intellectual sophistication, it is still the activity by means of which our sensation is kept alert, our imagination kept vivid, our power of reasoning kept keen. The mind sinks into apathy unless its hungry roots are continuously searching the dark sustenance of the unknown, its sensitive foliage continuously stretching towards unimaginable light.[32]

Quite unlike the aesthetes and possibly the formalists, who felt that the capacity for disinterested aesthetic experience is always limited to a small segment of society, Read is convinced of the universality of aesthetic experience. The absence of a capacity for aesthetic experience is not innate in the individual, but is invariably the result of repression by a society whose norms exclude the free expression of aesthetic impulses.

My emphasis on Read's aesthetics in relation to his criticism, while undoubtedly relevant to his sociological theories, may give a distorted view of his total achievement as a writer on art. Read's present reputation as a critic rests on his success as an exponent of modern art, but, since taste is notoriously unstable, it is very likely that he will be known best by *Art and Society, Art and Industry, The Grass Roots of Art,* and primarily by *Education Through Art.* In all these works, Read continued the task of examining the interactions of art and human conduct which had been inaugurated by Ruskin. Except in the broadest areas, Read's views do not coincide with those of Ruskin. He concurs in the belief that the quality of a society is necessarily reflected in its art, but is unable to subscribe to most of Ruskin's practical prescriptions for the reformation of English art and society. Ruskin's sociology was predominantly deterministic; he believed that economic organization was the key to aesthetic production and that in order to establish a society in which both beauty and virtue would flourish, it was necessary to abandon industrialism and return to the handicraft system. Incidentally, Ruskin's preoccupation with the sociology of art and eventually with political economy contributed to the deterioration of his critical capacity, particularly with respect to the art of his own time. Read is in accord with Ruskin's hatred of the ugliness and brutality wrought by industrialism, but he does not share Ruskin's belief in the incompatibility of art and the machine. *Art and Industry,* Read's most un-Ruskinian work, takes sharp issue with Ruskin on aesthetic grounds. Whereas Ruskin and his disciple, William Morris, were activated by the most admirable motives, their opposition to the machine was not only impractical but also mistaken, since it was based on an exclusive conception of art as humanistic, that is, as concerned with the expression of human ideals and emotions in plastic form. They were unable to recognize abstract or nonfigurative art, which has as its sole aim the making of objects whose appeal is wholly aesthetic. According to Read, design rather than execution is the paramount consideration; the final product of the machine, when designed or determined by one who is sensitive to formal values, becomes an abstract work of art in the subtler sense of the term. Read pleads for a broader concept of art which would include typewriters, gasoline pumps, refrigerators, vacuum cleaners—all articles of use, in fact, which are capable of being submitted to the discipline of form and its accompanying grace or harmony.

In *Art and Industry,* Read establishes beyond doubt the validity of claiming aesthetic merit for machine-made products, but he does not deal with the problem which lies at the heart of Ruskin's attack on industrialism, the moral and social effects of a system which deprives the individual worker of the satisfactions of spontaneous creative activity. *The Grass Roots of Art* takes full account of Ruskin's argument as well as of the inevitability of industrialism:

Only a people serving an apprenticeship to nature can be trusted with machines. Only such people will so contrive good control of these machines that their products are an enhancement of biological needs, and not a denial of them. Only such a people with sensations still vivid and intelligence ever active, can hope to form a stable and integrated society in the industrial world of the future.[33]

The practical solution envisages a "double-decker civilization" in which every individual destined to industrial labor would serve an apprenticeship in handicrafts. Read goes much further than this, actually, warning that the only alternative to the vast neurosis that has overtaken a mechanized and rationalized civilization is a society in which all members realize their artistic potentialities.

The reference to neurosis reveals the psychological bias not only of Read's social and political views but also of his aesthetics. In the long run his views on art and society are integral with the notion of the biological foundations of human activity. In the broadest sense of the term, this is an ethical notion. But Read is explicit in avoiding the idea of a simple or direct equivalence of art and morality as well as the procedure of judging art according to an a priori ethical system. He maintains that art performs its ethical function precisely by preserving its independence of ideological motives. In asserting that the specifically ethical aspect of art resides in its formal characteristics rather than in the nature of its subject matter, Read disassociates himself completely from the prevailing nineteenth-century attitude:

The ethical aspect of art was one of the preoccupations of nineteenth-century writers, and from Ruskin to Tolstoy they all made a desperate effort to give art an ethical foundation. . . . They had only one notion of how this could be done. . . . The artist himself must have an ethical conception of life and must give clear expression to it in his works. But art remained obstinately non-ethical; indeed these doctrines only succeeded in provoking a reaction among artists, and art has never been so deliberately devoid of message as during the last fifty years. At the same time, and in the true sense of the word, we can also assert that art has never been so effectively ethical. . . . For art actually becomes more ethical the purer it becomes.[34]

Read's argument on behalf of the social function of art embodies this idea. In *Art and Society,* the autonomy of art itself and of the artist as individual is defended against the deterministic and reductive tendencies of historical criticism. Read is willing to concede that the formal structure of art is modified by the practices of magic, religion, science, and politics, but not that it is actually determined by them in the sense that art is a by-product of culture and society. Written during the decade in which the prestige of Marxist criticism was at its height, the book relies on a Freudian approach to counteract the excesses of a socioeconomic interpretation of art. Read ascribes the social value of art to its cognitive role, which is in itself morally significant:

> The artist, we have admitted, is a unit of a necessary social organization and cannot arrive even at the threshold of his potentialities without conditions which a culture provides. But having reached that threshold, he must be left to proceed alone as an individual. . . . Across the threshold is the subliminal self; a self which is more than the conscious entity of the ego, limited as that is by all the restrictions and conventions of the compromise we call civilization; a self which is in fact another order of reality, profounder and more extensive than any known to our daily perceptions. It is just because the artist can cross that threshold into that more extensive realm and bring back some knowledge of its meaning that he is supreme among his fellow men.[35]

At this stage, Read was inclined to be ultraromantic, emphasizing the uniqueness of genius and the inherent opposition between the artist and his society. His later insights into the relations of art and society are based on a view which does not revoke the idea of the unconscious as the source of artistic activity, to be sure, but nevertheless puts less stress on the extraordinary nature of that activity than on the universality of aesthetic capability and consequently on art as a discipline affecting all men and involving the whole personality. His politics have shifted meanwhile from the defense of the artist's freedom against the tyranny of a coercive society to the reformation of society itself, not primarily by political or economic measures, but by means of the recognition of the nature of personality. The principal agent of social regeneration is the radical theory of education expounded in *Education Through Art,* which represents a summation of Read's aesthetic and social philosophy. The idea linking together the realms of art and society is the organic nature of each. The qualities that characterize a genuine culture—

spontaneity, variety, and freedom—are precisely those which
are found in art. There is no longer a question of the separation of artist and society, or indeed of art and life, for Read
maintains that the principle of life itself is aesthetic by virtue
of its embodiment of energy in a form which is not merely
material but aesthetic.

The principal object of Read's attack is the post-Renaissance civilization of the Western world and more specifically
the educational theory which fostered that civilization. The
destructive effect of traditional education theory on the personality is twofold. It emphasizes the logico-rational aspect
of intellectual life to the total neglect of the sensuous and
aesthetic basis of mental activity. It imposes, furthermore, a
totally erroneous conception of the uniformity of personality
which inhibits individual spontaneity and creativity.

Since Read's aim is definitely not the development of
aesthetic awareness as an end in itself, but the moral and intellectual well-being of mankind, it is fitting that his educational theory takes its point of departure from Plato, who
declares the aesthetic basis of ethics: "He said, as the modern
psychologist says, that all grace of movement and harmony
of living—the moral disposition of the soul itself—are determined by aesthetic feeling; by the recognition of rhythm
and harmony. . . ." [36] The key term in Read's development
of the idea of personality is "integration," by which he
means something closely allied to the organization of the
biological organism:

Civilization produces a split consciousness, a world made up of
discordant forces, a world of images divorced from reality, of
concepts divorced from sensation, of logic divorced from life. At
best we can recover an integrated consciousness in our art, but
even our art has been invaded by intellectual attitudes which
destroy its organic vitality. The argument of this book is that the
purpose of education, as of art, should be to preserve the organic
wholeness of man and of his mental facilities, so that as he passes

from childhood to manhood, from savagery to civilization, he nevertheless retains the unity of consciousness which is the only source of social harmony and individual happiness.[37]

One of Read's favorite expressions is "the innocent eye," the title of his autobiography. The conception of personality on which his theory of education is based is obviously related to romantic psychology and philosophy. But his educational program could not have come into being without the great interest in children's art which has taken place in the present century, as well as in primitive art. For Read, children's art is the truest index of personality:

The art of the child declines after the age of eleven because it is attacked from every direction—squeezed out of the mind by logical activities. The price we pay for this distortion of the adolescent mind is mounting up: a civilization of hideous objects and misshapen human beings, of sick minds and unhappy households, of divided societies armed with weapons of mass destruction. We feed these processes of dissolution with our knowledge and science, with our inventions and discoveries, and our educational system tries to keep pace with the holocaust; but the creative activities which could heal the mind and make beautiful our environment, unite man with nature and nation with nation—these we dismiss as idle, irrelevant and inane.[38]

The signal importance of art in the educational process is the necessity for spontaneous creative activity. Contrary to the normal approach which forces the mind of the individual into a preconceived mold, the method advocated by Read takes full account of the diversity of temperament which has been fully reflected for the first time in the phenomenon of modern art, partly because of the existence of free, democratic societies in Europe and the United States for the past century and a half. It might be objected that Read's program belongs to the realm of mental therapy and "personality development" rather than to the cultivation of the mind, which has been the traditional aim of education. This is a distinction which Read would disavow since, as we have already seen in connection with his aesthetic theory, he regards aesthetic activity as an essential part of the mind itself, indeed that part of the mind from which conceptual thought originated. Accordingly, the purpose of an aesthetically oriented education is not to produce professional artists, but simply the exercise and training of the senses lacking which man is unable to achieve the wholeness or integration required by both the individual and his society. The social importance of art itself, the product of exceptionally gifted individuals which is indeed highly prized in our culture, rests in part upon its intimate relationship with those universal and instinctive aesthetic potentialities which society neglects or suppresses at its own peril.

# Notes

## JOHN RUSKIN

[1] E. H. Gombrich, *Art and Illusion* (New York: Pantheon, 1960), p. 14.

[2] John Ruskin, *Works*, XI, p. 201; *The Stones of Venice*, III. (First published in 1851–1853.)

[3] Graham Hough, *The Last Romantics* (London: Gerald Duckworth, 1949), p. xvii.

[4] J. M. Brydon, in the Introduction to John Ruskin, *The Seven Lamps of Architecture, Works*, VIII (London, 1903), p. xliii.

[5] Virginia Woolf, *Roger Fry* (New York: Harcourt, Brace, 1940), p. 280.

[6] Ruskin, *Works*, V, pp. 38–39; *Modern Painters*, III.

[7] *Works*, IV, p. 26; *Modern Painters*, II.

[8] Joan Evans, *John Ruskin* (New York: Oxford, 1954), pp. 411–412.

[9] Ruskin, *Works*, IV, p. 35; *Modern Painters*, II.

[10] Ruskin, *Works*, VIII, p. xxvi; *The Stones of Venice*, II.

[11] Ruskin, *Works*, III, p. xxxix; *Modern Painters*, I.

[12] Marcel Proust, *La Bible d'Amiens*, quoted in Walter A. Strauss, *Proust and Literature* (Cambridge, Mass.: Harvard, 1957), p. 80.

[13] Ruskin, *Works*, III, p. xxii; *Modern Painters*, I.

[14] *Works*, III, p. 137; *Modern Painters*, I.

[15] *Works*, III, pp. 104–105; *Modern Painters*, I.

[16] *Works*, IV, p. 250; *Modern Painters*, II.

[17] Charles Baudelaire, "L'Art philosophique," quoted in *The Mirror of Art*, ed. by J. Mayne (New York: Doubleday, 1956), p. xvii.

[18] *Ibid.*, p. 279.

[19] Quoted in L. Venturi, *History of Art Criticism* (New York: E. P. Dutton, 1936), p. 251.

[20] Ruskin, *Works*, III, p. 193; *Modern Painters*, I.

[21] *Works*, VI, p. 187; *Modern Painters*, IV.

[22] *Works*, III, p. 87; *Modern Painters*, I.

[23] *Works*, IV, p. 204; *Modern Painters*, II.

[24] *Ibid.*, p. 224.

[25] Geoffrey Scott, *The Architecture of Humanism* (New York: Doubleday, 1954), p. 105.

[26] Ruskin, *Works*, VIII, p. 218; *The Seven Lamps of Architecture.*

[27] Ruskin, *Works*, X, p. 192; *The Stones of Venice*, II.
[28] *Ibid.*, pp. 193–194.
[29] *Works*, XI, p. 46; *The Stones of Venice*, III.
[30] *Ibid.*, p. 49.
[31] *Ibid.*, p. 49.
[32] *Ibid.*, p. 66.
[33] *Works*, X, p. 216; *The Stones of Venice*, II.
[34] Joan Evans, *John Ruskin*, pp. 413–414.

## WALTER PATER

[1] Iain Fletcher, *Walter Pater*, Writers and Their Work series, no. 114 (London: Longmans, Green, 1959), p. 36.
[2] Quoted in Sylvia Sprigge, *Berenson: A Biography* (Boston: Houghton Mifflin, 1960), p. 48.
[3] Walter Pater, *The Renaissance* (London: Macmillan, 1888), p. x.
[4] Walter Pater, "Style," *Appreciations* (London: Macmillan, 1897), p. 14.
[5] Pater, *The Renaissance*, p. 103.
[6] *Ibid.*, p. 129.
[7] *Ibid.*, pp. xi–xii.
[8] *Ibid.*, p. 252.
[9] *Ibid.*, p. 2.
[10] *Ibid.*, p. 193.
[11] *Ibid.*, p. 234.
[12] *Ibid.*, p. 116.
[13] *Ibid.*, p. 57.
[14] A. C. Benson, *Walter Pater* (New York: Macmillan, 1906), p. 185.
[15] *Ibid.*, p. 206.
[16] Pater, *The Renaissance*, p. 67.
[17] *Ibid.*, p. ix.
[18] *Ibid.*, p. 75.
[19] *Ibid.*, p. 69.
[20] Pater, *Appreciations*, p. 6.
[21] *Ibid.*, pp. 80–81.
[22] *Ibid.*, p. 35.
[23] Pater, *The Renaissance*, p. 135.
[24] *Ibid.*, pp. 136–137.
[25] *Ibid.*, p. 140.
[26] *Ibid.*, p. 145.

## CLIVE BELL

[1] Clive Bell, *Art*, 2nd edition (London: Chatto and Windus, 1920), pp. 76–82.
[2] *Ibid.*, p. 158.

[3] Clive Bell, *Enjoying Pictures* (London: Chatto and Windus, 1934), pp. 15–16.

[4] Clive Bell, *Since Cézanne*, 2nd edition (London: Chatto and Windus, 1929), pp. 99–100.

[5] Bell, *Art*, pp. 6–8.

[6] *Ibid.*, p. 28.

[7] *Ibid.*, p. 39.

[8] *Ibid.*, pp. 158–160.

[9] *Ibid.*, pp. 207–209.

[10] Bell, *Since Cézanne*, pp. 36–37.

## ROGER FRY

[1] Roger Fry, *French, Flemish and British Art* (New York: Coward-McCann, 1951), pp. 41–42. (A collection of three series of lectures.)

[2] *Ibid.*, pp. 188–189.

[3] Roger Fry, *Vision and Design*, 1st American edition (New York: Brentano's, 1924), p. 285.

[4] *Ibid.*, p. 131.

[5] *Ibid.*, pp. 168–169.

[6] *Ibid.*, p. 142.

[7] *Ibid.*, p. 27.

[8] *Ibid.*, p. 28.

[9] *Ibid.*, p. 29.

[10] *Ibid.*, p. 36.

[11] *Ibid.*, p. 33.

[12] *Ibid.*, p. 294.

[13] *Ibid.*, p. 302.

[14] *Ibid.*, p. 301.

[15] Roger Fry, *Transformations* (New York: Brentano's, 1926), p. 3.

[16] *Ibid.*, p. 10.

[17] *Ibid.*, p. 19.

[18] *Ibid.*, p. 20.

[19] *Ibid.*, p. 38.

[20] *Ibid.*, p. 42.

[21] *Ibid.*, p. 26.

[22] Roger Fry, *Cézanne* (New York: Macmillan, 1927), p. 69.

[23] Roger Fry, *Architectural Heresies of a Painter* (London: Chatto and Windus, 1921).

[24] Fry, *Cézanne*, pp. 37–38.

[25] *Ibid.*, pp. 39–40.

[26] Fry, *French, Flemish and British Art*, p. 20.

[27] Fry, *Vision and Design*, p. 178.

[28] Fry, *Transformations*, p. 201.

[29] Roger Fry, *Last Lectures* (New York: Macmillan, 1939), p. 12.

# NOTES

Ibid., p. 13.

Ibid., p. 19.

Ibid., pp. 28–29.

Ibid., pp. 114–116.

Ibid., p. 45.

Fry, *Transformations*, p. 185.

Ibid., p. 187.

## HERBERT READ

[1] Herbert Read, *A Coat of Many Colours* (London: Routledge, 1945), p. 283.

[2] Ibid., p. 191.

[3] Herbert Read, *The Philosophy of Modern Art*, 2nd edition (London: Faber and Faber, 1954), p. 261.

[4] Herbert Read, *Art Now*, 2nd edition (London: Faber and Faber, 1948), p. 32.

[5] Sir Joshua Reynolds, *Third Discourse*, quoted in *Art Now*, pp. 34-35.

[6] Read, *Art Now*, p. 37.

[7] Herbert Read, *Henry Moore* (London: Percy Lund, Humphries, 1957), p. xi.

[8] Herbert Read, *The Tenth Muse* (London: Routledge and Kegan Paul, 1957), p. 163.

[9] Read, *The Philosophy of Modern Art*, pp. 156–157.

[10] Herbert Read, *The Meaning of Art* (Baltimore: Penguin Books, 1959), p. 21.

[11] Read, *The Philosophy of Modern Art*, p. 13.

[12] Read, *The Tenth Muse*, p. 173.

[13] Read, *Art Now*, p. 69.

[14] Read, *The Philosophy of Modern Art*, pp. 82–83.

[15] Herbert Read, *The Grass Roots of Art* (New York: Wittenborn, 1947), p. 10.

[16] Herbert Read, *A Coat of Many Colours*, pp. 80–81.

[17] Herbert Read, *Icon and Idea* (London: Faber and Faber, 1955), p. 32.

[18] Read, *Henry Moore*, pp. xiii-xvi.

[19] Herbert Read, *The Art of Sculpture* (New York: Pantheon, 1956), pp. 121–122.

[20] Read, *A Coat of Many Colours*, p. 82.

[21] Read, *The Tenth Muse*, pp. 29–30.

[22] Read, *The Philosophy of Modern Art*, p. 24.

[23] Ibid., p. 41.

[24] Read, *Icon and Idea*, p. 18.

[25] Ibid., p. 20.

[26] Ibid., p. 5.

[27] Ibid., p. 50.

[28] *Ibid.*, p. 32.

[29] *Ibid.*, p. 74.

[30] *Ibid.*, p. 87.

[31] *Ibid.*, pp. 129–130.

[32] *Ibid.*, p. 32.

[33] Read, *The Grass Roots of Art*, p. 92.

[34] Read, *A Coat of Many Colours*, pp. 205–206.

[35] Herbert Read, *Art and Society*, 2nd edition (New York: Pantheon, 1945), p. 80.

[36] Herbert Read, *Education Through Art* (London: Faber and Faber, 1948), p. 62.

[37] *Ibid.*, p. 68.

[38] *Ibid.*, p. 168–169.

# Index

# INDEX

Fry, Roger, 1, 2, 3, 4, 7, 17, 27, 41, 72, 147–152, 158, 161, 162, 168, 170, 172; aestheticism, 107–108; Post-Impressionism, 109–110; significant form, 110–112; "Giotto," 112–116; "Essay on Aesthetics," 122–128; Cézanne, 130–131; plastic form, 131–134; "Last Lectures," 135–139; Expressionism, 139–141

Gabo, Naum, 98, 167, 178
Gauguin, 99, 172
Géricault, 98
Ghirlandajo, 24
Gill, Eric, 3
Giorgione, 66–71, 76, 157
Giotto, 24, 41, 71, 90, 96, 110, 112–114, 116, 118
Gombrich, E. H., 16
Goncourts, the, 2
Gothic art, 36, 37, 39, 90, 153, 163
Gris, Juan, 178
Grünewald, 139
Guardi, 92
Guillaumin, 131

Hazlitt, William, 3
Hildebrand, 119
Hobbema, 21
Hogarth, 3, 92
Hough, Graham, 16, 26
Hulme, T. E., 154

Impressionist school, 23, 169
Ingres, 51, 98

James, Henry, 1
Johnson, Lionel, 47
Jordaens, 92
Jung, Carl, 160

Kafka, Franz, 57
Kandinsky, 169
Klee, Paul, 162, 170, 171
Kokoschka, 170

Langer, Suzanne, 97
Legros, 51
Lessing, Gotthold, 67
Löwenfeld, Viktor, 163

Mallarmé, 115
Malraux, André, 2, 17, 76, 170

Manet, 130
Mantegna, 91
Masaccio, 91, 177
Masolino, 91
Matisse, 94, 151, 161
Michelangelo, 50, 54, 58, 63, 132
"Mona Lisa" ("La Giaconda"), 52–53, 63, 113
Mondrian, 98, 178
Moore, George, 3, 51, 106
Moore, Henry, 57, 167, 171
Morris, William, 3, 79, 109, 180

Neolithic art, 163, 174–175, 176
Newton, Eric, 3
Nicholson, Ben, 165–166, 167, 170
Nietzsche, 152–153

Orcagna, 24

Paleolithic art, 163, 174–175, 176
Pater, Walter, 1, 2, 4, 6, 7, 76–78, 96, 108, 147, 150, 156; aestheticism, 47–50; contemporary art, 51; impressionist criticism, 52–53; ethics, 55–56; decadence, 57–58; influence of Ruskin, 60–61; romantic expressionism, 61–63; "Style," 64–66; formalism, 67–71
Pattison, Mrs. Mark, 49
Picasso, 57, 94, 151, 152, 170
Pissarro, 131
Pliny, 16
Post-Impressionism, 18, 87, 89, 96, 109–110, 114, 120, 122, 141, 147
Poussin, 20, 28, 92, 125, 132
Pre-Raphaelites, 21, 24, 109
Proust, 2, 25, 57

Raphael, 95, 96
Read, Herbert, 1, 4, 7, 18–19, 31, 57, 72, 79; pluralism, 148–149; the romantic principle, 152–154; on Ruskin, 155–156; formalism, 156–159; the unconscious, 160–161; psychology of forms, 161–164; naturalism, 165–166; art and cognition, 168–173; art and consciousness, 174–179; art and society, 179–183; art and education, 183–186
Rembrandt, 92, 110, 116, 125